AF740355

Sports Economics, Management and Policy

Series Editor

Dennis Coates

More information about this series at http://www.springer.com/series/8343

Thomas A. Rhoads

The Call Up to the Majors

A Proximity-Based Approach to the Economics of Minor League Baseball

Springer

Thomas A. Rhoads
Department of Economics
Towson University
Towson, MD, USA

ISSN 2191-298X ISSN 2191-2998 (electronic)
Sports Economics, Management and Policy
ISBN 978-1-4614-8923-8 ISBN 978-1-4614-8924-5 (eBook)
DOI 10.1007/978-1-4614-8924-5

Library of Congress Control Number: 2015934599

Springer New York Heidelberg Dordrecht London
© Springer Science+Business Media New York 2015
This work is subject to copyright. All rights are reserved by the Publisher, whether the whole or part of the material is concerned, specifically the rights of translation, reprinting, reuse of illustrations, recitation, broadcasting, reproduction on microfilms or in any other physical way, and transmission or information storage and retrieval, electronic adaptation, computer software, or by similar or dissimilar methodology now known or hereafter developed.
The use of general descriptive names, registered names, trademarks, service marks, etc. in this publication does not imply, even in the absence of a specific statement, that such names are exempt from the relevant protective laws and regulations and therefore free for general use.
The publisher, the authors and the editors are safe to assume that the advice and information in this book are believed to be true and accurate at the date of publication. Neither the publisher nor the authors or the editors give a warranty, express or implied, with respect to the material contained herein or for any errors or omissions that may have been made.

Printed on acid-free paper

Springer Science+Business Media LLC New York is part of Springer Science+Business Media (www.springer.com)

To Katelyn, Ben, and Allison.
Play hard and have fun!

Preface

From the comfort of my own home, my television gives me an opportunity to watch a seemingly unlimited number of baseball games on any given summer evening. Using my remote control and sometimes my laptop or Roku for assistance, I can relax on my couch and watch just about any full-season professional baseball game that I want. The fact that my home is located in Maryland impacts the way I watch (and pay for watching) just a few of those baseball games—I need a sports package with a cable or satellite provider to watch Baltimore Orioles or Washington Nationals games. Otherwise, the live baseball games available to me to watch on my television are precisely the same as anybody living just about anywhere else in the world.

The picture changes considerably, however, if I want to go to a stadium, buy a ticket, and watch a professional baseball game in person. Limiting myself to a drive that would take no more than about two hours or so, I have the option of attending a game at one of 16 professional baseball stadiums that are within a 100-mile radius of my home. Better understanding the value of having the option to comfortably attend a baseball game at one of these 16 baseball stadiums does not mean comparing that experience with the opportunity to watch the nearly unlimited amount of games available on my television. Just about anybody with a television and a high-speed Internet connection can watch just about any professional baseball game in their own home. And even though watching a baseball game on television and watching the same game at the stadium are close substitutes, they are sufficiently different entertainment options for most people and should be considered separately.

Instead, it is helpful for me to take note of the number of baseball stadiums within a 100-mile radius of my home and realize (rather quickly) that I am one of the fortunate few baseball fans with more than just a handful of available game-day stadium options. Notably, I have many more available options to attend a full-season professional baseball game based on where I live than many other people who also live in the US. For instance, someone living in the fifth largest metropolitan area in the US—Houston, Texas—has just two baseball stadiums located within a 100-mile radius. Minute Maid

Park in Houston is where Major League Baseball's Astros play their home games and Constellation Field in Sugar Land, Texas, is the home field for the Skeeters of the Atlantic League, an independent league team that has only been in existence since 2012. Without comparing the quality of the teams, the stadiums, parking, concessions, or the game-time experience in the Houston area to what I have available close to my home in Maryland, I am comfortable in claiming that having 16 possible stadiums and professional baseball teams to choose from is preferred by nearly all baseball fans to having only two possible stadiums and teams to choose from.

In fact, there are not many locations within the US that provide such a large number of professional baseball game options as I have available to me from my home in Maryland. The antitrust exemption that was granted in 1922 by the US Supreme Court to Major League Baseball and is effectively extended to its affiliated minor league teams largely dictates that most baseball fans in the US will have a somewhat limited number of choices of full-season professional baseball games to attend on any given day. Of course, this is by design—a limited choice set of games to attend at the stadium for the consumer leads to pricing power for owners and ownership groups. The literature is deep and rich here, as much has already been written on this subject.

However, given the wealth of options available to the baseball fan on television and the relatively low number of games for most baseball fans to attend at a stadium near their home, a natural question arises. Does proximity matter any more in the professional baseball industry? This question may not seem important given the multibillion dollar television deals that Major League Baseball and other top professional sports leagues have made in recent years. But professional baseball games are still played in stadiums in front of paying fans. In fact, quite a bit of research has already examined how decisions by baseball executives impact attendance at the stadium.

Even so, there is another element to the proximity of professional baseball teams that has largely been ignored in the economics literature. Namely, developing player talent for a Major League Baseball team typically means developing that talent at an affiliated minor league baseball team. That player development strategy is likely to be optimized when affiliated minor league baseball teams are in closer proximity to the parent Major League Baseball team and to the other affiliated minor league teams in the same organization. And herein lies the trade-off that makes the matter of proximity within minor league baseball interesting to study—closer minor league baseball teams make player development progress optimally while simultaneously leading to less pricing power for owners and ownership groups of professional baseball teams. Taking note of this trade-off and beginning to get a handle on how closely minor league baseball teams are located in comparison to each other, to their affiliated parent Major League Baseball team, and to the other minor league teams within that organization is the main reason for me writing this book.

Ultimately, proximity matters in minor league baseball. It is my goal that this book will open up new ways to study minor league baseball, specifically, and sports leagues more generally. So even as advanced technology has eliminated some of the need to be in close proximity to the teams that fans love to follow, there is still a need to understand more completely how proximity matters can impact the way sports leagues are structured and how that structure can ultimately impact the quality of the games that entertain increasingly enthusiastic sports fans across the country.

Towson, MD, USA Thomas A. Rhoads

Locations of Affiliated and Independent League Baseball Teams

N
CANADA
WA
Seattle Mariners
Tacoma Rainiers
MT
OR
ID
WY
Sacramento River Cats
Reno Aces
Salt Lake Bees
San Francisco Giants
Stockton Ports
NV
Oakland Athletics
Modesto Nuts
UT
Colordao Rockies
San Jose Giants
Colorado Springs Sky Sox
Fresno Grizzlies
CA
CO
Visalia Rawhide
Las Vegas 51s
Bakersfield Blaze
Lancaster JetHawks
High Desert Mavericks
Rancho Cucamonga Quakes
Inland Empire 66ers
Los Angeles Dodgers
Albuquerque Isotopes
Lake Elsinore Storm
AZ
Los Angeles Angels
San Diego Padres
NM
Arizona Diamondbacks
PACIFIC OCEAN
El Paso Chihuahuas
MEXICO
MLB
Triple A
Double A
Class A Advanced
Class A
Independent League

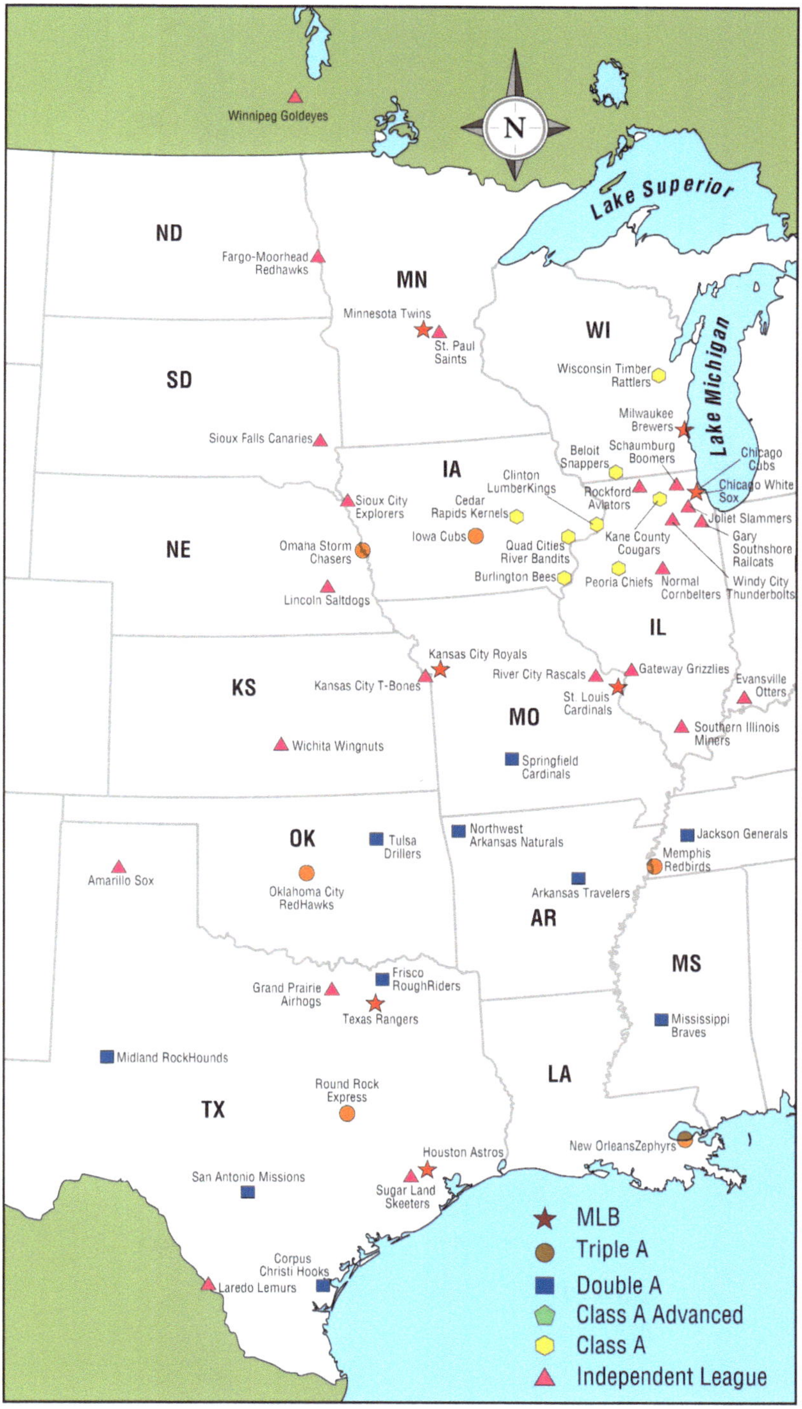
N
Lake Superior
Lake Michigan
Winnipeg Goldeyes
ND
Fargo-Moorhead Redhawks
MN
Minnesota Twins
St. Paul Saints
SD
Sioux Falls Canaries
WI
Wisconsin Timber Rattlers
Milwaukee Brewers
Beloit Snappers
Schaumburg Boomers
Chicago Cubs
Chicago White Sox
IA
Clinton LumberKings
Rockford Aviators
Sioux City Explorers
Cedar Rapids Kernels
Iowa Cubs
Kane County Cougars
Joliet Slammers
Gary Southshore Railcats
NE
Omaha Storm Chasers
Quad Cities River Bandits
Burlington Bees
Peoria Chiefs
Normal Cornbelters
Windy City Thunderbolts
Lincoln Saltdogs
IL
Kansas City Royals
KS
Kansas City T-Bones
River City Rascals
Gateway Grizzlies
Evansville Otters
St. Louis Cardinals
MO
Southern Illinois Miners
Wichita Wingnuts
Springfield Cardinals
OK
Tulsa Drillers
Northwest Arkansas Naturals
Jackson Generals
Memphis Redbirds
Amarillo Sox
Oklahoma City RedHawks
Arkansas Travelers
AR
MS
Frisco RoughRiders
Grand Prairie Airhogs
Texas Rangers
Mississippi Braves
Midland RockHounds
LA
Round Rock Express
TX
New OrleansZephyrs
Houston Astros
San Antonio Missions
Sugar Land Skeeters
Corpus Christi Hooks
Laredo Lemurs
MLB
Triple A
Double A
Class A Advanced
Class A
Independent League

N
Quebec Capitales
Trois-Rivieres Aigles
ME
VT
NH
Portland Sea Dogs
New Hampshire Fisher Cats
MA
RI
CT
NY
Lake Ontario
Toronto Blue Jays
Lake Huron
Lake Michigan
Traverse City Beach Bums
Great Lakes Loons
MI
Lansing Lugnuts
West Michigan Whitecaps
Detroit Tigers
Lake Erie
Lake County Captains
Cleveland Indians
PA
Toledo Mud Hens
Lake Erie Crushers
Akron RubberDucks
NJ
South Bend Cubs
Fort Wayne TinCaps
OH
Columbus Clippers
DE
IN
Indianapolis Indians
Dayton Dragons
Potomac Nationals
MD
WV
Cincinnati Reds
Florence Freedom
West Virginia Power
Lynchburg Hillcats
VA
Richmond Flying Squirrels
Norfolk Tides
Lexington Legends
Salem Red Sox
Evansville Otters
Louisville Bats
KY
Carolina Mudcats
Winston-Salem Dash
ATLANTIC OCEAN
Bowling Green Hot Rods
NC
Durham Bulls
Greensboro Grasshoppers
Tennessee Smokies
Hickory Crawdads
Kannapolis Intimidators
Nashville Sounds
TN
Asheville Tourists
Charlotte Knights
Chattanooga Lookouts
Greenville Drive
Myrtle Beach Pelicans
Gwinnett Braves
Huntsville Stars
Rome Braves
SC
Atlanta Braves
Augusta GreenJackets
Charleston RiverDogs
MLB
Triple A
Double A
Class A Advanced
Class A
Independent League
Birmingham Barons
AL
GA
Savannah Sand Gnats
Montgomery Biscuits
Mobile BayBears
Jacksonville Suns
Pensacola Blue Wahoos
Daytona Cubs
FL
Lakeland Flying Tigers
Tampa Yankees
Brevard County Manatees
Dunedin Blue Jays
Clearwater Threshers
Bradenton Marauders
Tampa Bay Rays
St. Lucie Mets
Jupiter Hammerheads
Palm Beach Cardinals
Charlotte Stone Crabs
Fort Myers Miracle
BAHAMAS
Miami Marlins
Gulf of Mexico

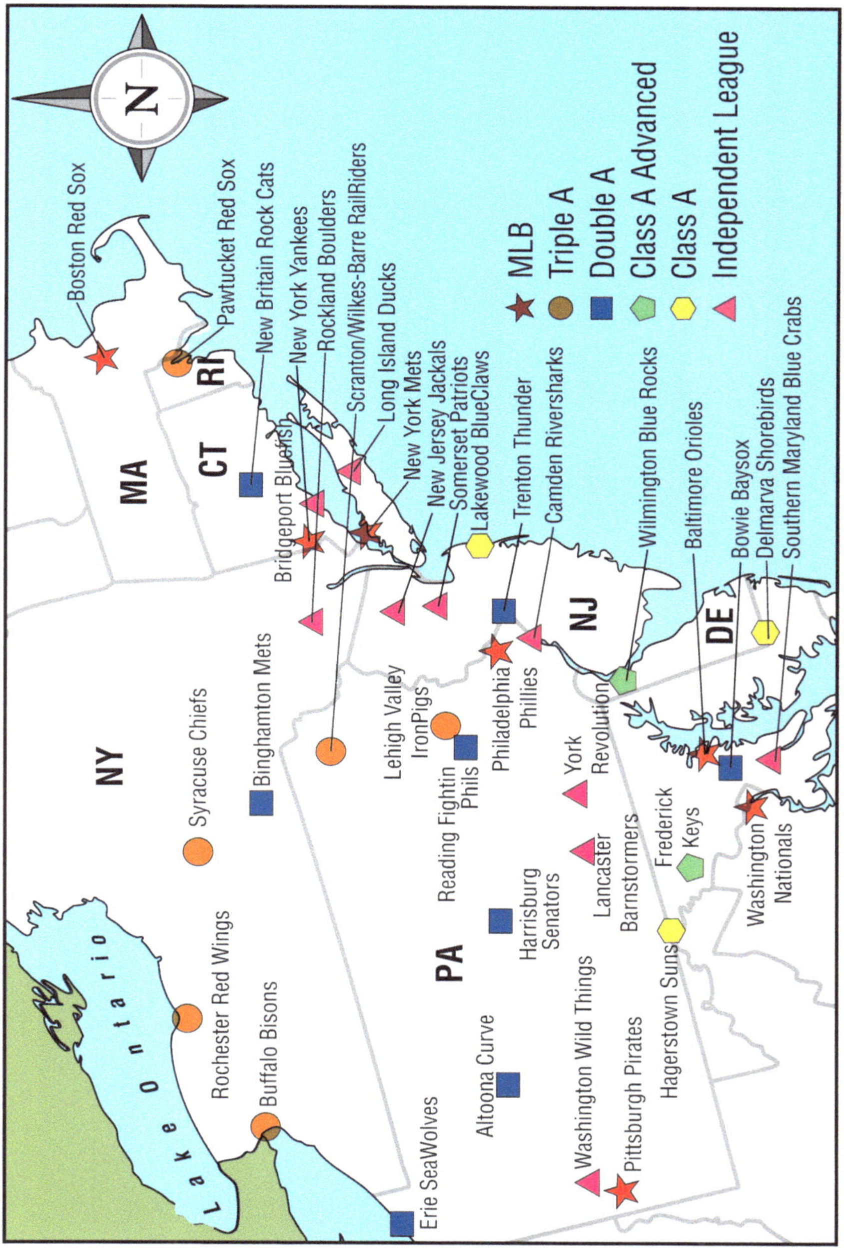
N
Boston Red Sox
Pawtucket Red Sox
New Britain Rock Cats
New York Yankees
Rockland Boulders
Scranton/Wilkes-Barre RailRiders
Long Island Ducks
New York Mets
New Jersey Jackals
Somerset Patriots
Lakewood BlueClaws
Trenton Thunder
Camden Riversharks
Wilmington Blue Rocks
Baltimore Orioles
Bowie Baysox
Delmarva Shorebirds
Southern Maryland Blue Crabs
MLB
Triple A
Double A
Class A Advanced
Class A
Independent League
MA
CT
RI
NY
NJ
DE
PA
Bridgeport Bluefish
Syracuse Chiefs
Binghamton Mets
Lehigh Valley IronPigs
Reading Fightin Phils
Philadelphia Phillies
York Revolution
Harrisburg Senators
Lancaster Barnstormers
Frederick Keys
Washington Nationals
Hagerstown Suns
Altoona Curve
Washington Wild Things
Pittsburgh Pirates
Rochester Red Wings
Buffalo Bisons
Erie SeaWolves
Lake Ontario

Acknowledgements

A few people must be singled out for helping in various and unique ways with my completing this project. First, I want to thank Dennis Coates for thinking highly enough of my work to even consider asking me to write a book on minor league baseball. Thanks especially to Seth Gitter, without whom my work would not be considered at all. Thanks to the College of Business and Economics at Towson University for giving me the time to write this book. Thanks to my editor, Lorraine Klimowich, for pushing me without being pushy. And thanks to Susan Westendorf and others at Springer for making this book look and feel exactly how I wanted it to look and feel. Finally, I need to thank my wife Melissa and our kids Katelyn, Ben, and Allison. The four of you give me more inspiration and motivation than you will ever know. You also give me four good reasons to go to as many baseball games as possible. I love you all!

Contents

Chapter 1
Proximity and Minor League Baseball

For the Major League Baseball fan, September is one of the more special times of the year. As the postseason picture begins to come into focus, fans can expect to witness much drama on the baseball field and in the standings. And even though October is generally known as the month for postseason heroics, tweaks to the Major League Baseball postseason dynamics—adding a divisional series and a wildcard—ostensibly allow more fans to have a deeper interest in the outcomes of regular season games in September.

But there is another event in the affiliated baseball world in September that attracts much less attention from baseball fans than the pennant race and nevertheless has the potential to have similarly long-lasting impacts on a Major League organization. The affiliation shuffle, as it is informally known, gives both Major League Baseball teams and minor league baseball teams the opportunity to end existing affiliations and form new ones. With an eye to the future, Major League Baseball teams sign Player Development Contracts, formally affiliating with minor league baseball teams to develop what they hope to be their next crop of players for their Major League team. Sometimes, the switches leading to the new affiliations are quite obvious. And sometimes, they are not. But in each affiliation switch, there is a reminder that affiliated professional baseball is a business, and decisions are made to impact the bottom line.

The Affiliation Shuffle

The most recent affiliation shuffle began in September 2014. One example of how complicated the shuffle can become starts with the Sacramento River Cats of the Pacific Coast League—the Oakland A's Triple A affiliate from 2000 until 2014. The River Cats signed a Player Development Contract to begin a new affiliation in 2015 with the San Francisco Giants, thus switching their affiliation to what many

© Springer Science+Business Media New York 2015

T.A. Rhoads, *The Call Up to the Majors*, Sports Economics, Management and Policy 7, DOI 10.1007/978-1-4614-8924-5_1

consider to be the more popular Bay Area Major League Baseball team. But because of the nature of affiliations between Major League Baseball teams and their minor league affiliates, it is impossible for just one Major League team to switch their affiliation with a minor league team without at least one other affiliation switch taking place.

In this case, the River Cats switch was just one of a series of other affiliation switches that could only be described as dizzying. The Oakland A's are now affiliated with the Nashville Sounds, who had been affiliated with the Milwaukee Brewers. Now, the Milwaukee Brewers are affiliated with the Colorado Springs Sky Sox, who had been affiliated with the Colorado Rockies since the Rockies became a Major League franchise. The Rockies are now affiliated with the Albuquerque Isotopes, who ended their affiliation with the Los Angeles Dodgers. The Dodgers are now affiliated with the Oklahoma City RedHawks.[1] This move was made after the Los Angeles Dodgers ownership group purchased the RedHawks. Finally, the shuffle ended when the Houston Astros, who had previously been affiliated with the RedHawks, became affiliated with the Fresno Grizzlies. The Grizzlies had been affiliated with the San Francisco Giants before the Giants switched their affiliation to the Sacramento River Cats. Indeed, when it comes to the affiliation shuffle, what goes around comes around.

Proximity Matters

No doubt, the business of professional affiliated baseball is not for anyone unwilling to make tough business decisions. Ownership at all levels of affiliated baseball is assumed to make all their business decisions—including affiliation decisions—with an eye towards turning a profit. This is nothing different from any other business decision made in any other business setting. But there is at least one affiliation switch in the series of switches described above that brings to light a very important matter—proximity—within professional baseball that has escaped much academic scrutiny until now.

The move by the Oakland A's to sign a Player Development Contract with the Nashville Sounds—a team nearly 2,000 miles away from Oakland, California—when the Fresno Grizzlies, a Triple A team in the same Pacific Coast League as the Sacramento River Cats and Nashville Sounds, is only 150 miles away is a puzzle. After all, opportunities to grow and maintain a strong regional fan base for the Major League Baseball team are made easier by having its Triple A affiliate located relatively close. And moving players up to a Major League Baseball team from a Triple A level team only 150 miles away can typically be done quickly and with relatively low cost. So it is curious when Billy Beane, the Oakland A's General Manager of Moneyball fame, said of the new affiliation with the Nashville Sounds

[1] Beginning in 2015, Oklahoma City's Triple A team will be known as the Dodgers, not the RedHawks.

that its location was "convenient for player movement."[2] There is likely a more detailed back story that is not available to the public, because it is hard to believe that a Triple A affiliate that is about 1,800 miles further away than another available affiliate in the same league at the same level is noted for making player movement a convenient exercise for the Major League team.

In any case, this episode does point out an obvious fact: proximity matters for a Major League Baseball team from a player development perspective. That is, moving players between levels is partly a function of the proximity between teams at all the levels of affiliated baseball. And if optimal player movement between levels of a Major League Baseball team could lead to maximizing player development opportunities, then proximity between levels of a Major League organization matters in building the best possible roster of Major League players.

Perhaps more than any other matter that arises in the business of baseball, proximity to other professional baseball teams is a concern that has uniquely shaped professional baseball in North America. In fact, it is this unique component in how professional baseball is organized that shapes the need for a proximity-based approach to studying the economics of minor league baseball. And that is precisely the focus of this book.

What Is a Proximity-Based Approach?

A proximity-based approach to studying minor league baseball puts location, or place, at the center of the analysis. It matters that the game of baseball is played in a stadium in front of fans. So the key feature in this book that distinguishes the research here from much of the existing research on minor league baseball is the motivating story—proximity matters. There are two primary reasons that make proximity a key component in the business of affiliated professional baseball. One reason can largely benefit minor league baseball teams and the other reason can largely benefit Major League Baseball teams. The core of this book provides more detailed empirical analysis of these issues. We briefly summarize each of these benefits here.

First, affiliated minor league baseball teams enjoy some of the benefits of the antitrust exemption status granted to Major League Baseball through the 1922 Supreme Court ruling in the Federal Baseball case.[3] Namely, Major League Baseball's antitrust exemption status allows Major League Baseball team owners to

[2] Billy Beane's comments appeared in "Change is all the rage in affiliation shifts," by Benjamin Hill and accessed at http://www.milb.com/news/article.jsp?ymd=20141002&content_id=97205032&fext=.jsp&vkey=min_bus&sid=milb on October 9, 2014.

[3] Many other books offer descriptions of the Federal Baseball case and how it leads to Major League Baseball's antitrust exemption. Andrew Zimbalist's take on the ruling in his 2003 book, May the Best Team Win: Baseball Economics and Public Policy, offers clear insight into this matter. I refer the reader to Zimbalist's book and others like it to get a better sense of how Major League Baseball received such a favorable Supreme Court ruling.

dictate with a great deal of authority where affiliated professional baseball teams at all levels locate. Because affiliated minor league baseball teams are included in the implementation of Major League Rule 52 that establishes the geographical territorial rights for both Major League and affiliated minor league teams, affiliated minor league baseball teams have at most limited competition from other affiliated professional baseball teams in selling tickets to their baseball games.

Second, Major League Baseball teams have the opportunity to sometimes affiliate with minor league baseball teams that are in relatively close proximity. Minor league teams that are in close proximity to the parent Major League team allow front-office staff personnel to observe player development progress more often as travel costs are lower. This can provide for an optimal player development strategy to be enforced. Additionally, minor league teams that are in close proximity to the other minor league baseball teams within the same organization provide for optimal player movement between levels of the Major League organization. Again, this can keep travel costs low when implementing an optimal strategy for player development. It must be assumed that for any given Major League Baseball team, an optimal set of affiliated minor league teams will be in close proximity to both the parent Major League team and to each of the other minor league teams within the same organization. This allows player development and player movement to progress in an optimal manner with little or no friction caused by travel costs.

Proximity and the Business of Baseball

In many ways, the business of professional baseball in America can be viewed as a primer on business in America. After nearly a century and a half of growth and development, professional baseball can be described as a well-established industry within the US that is at the same time both a reflection of the broader business climate in America and a picture of what businesses can become with little or no threat of government interference in the operational side of the business. It's no surprise, therefore, that in recent years professional baseball teams have taken advantage of new techniques and technologies that provide fans with a better experience at the ballpark. After all, maintaining or even growing an already sizable revenue stream demands precisely this. And at a very basic level, professional baseball teams are no different than most every other successful business in America seeking growth opportunities.

But there is one area that has seen a divergence of business practices between professional baseball and many other businesses in America. Namely, many other businesses have taken advantage of the technology that eliminates much of the need for customers to be in close proximity in time and space to the point of production and sale. The availability of high-speed Internet to a growing number of consumers in America has led to more and more opportunities to connect buyers and sellers across time and space. As technology advances, more opportunities exist to connect buyers and sellers without requiring them to meet together in both time and space.

Take as a simple example of how proximity is less important in driving retail sales in America during the all-important holiday shopping season. Black Friday—the day after Thanksgiving that is often noted as the beginning of the holiday shopping season—was traditionally seen as the bellwether of retail sales for the holiday shopping season. But more and more, Cyber Monday—the first Monday after Thanksgiving that is often marked as the start of the online holiday shopping season—is becoming just as much a part of the American experience in the holiday shopping season as Black Friday. This shift in how retail sales are generated is just one obvious example of how innovation in business is one of the major hallmarks of a growing business in America.

Professional baseball in America—and especially minor league baseball—is still limited in its business model. Even today, a strong revenue stream requires fans to attend baseball games at the stadium. Without fans paying for tickets, parking, concessions, and souvenirs, there is generally not enough revenue flowing into a minor league baseball team for it to remain financially viable. Despite the inability to use technology to match consumers and producers across time and space, there has been an intriguing development in minor league baseball over the past 15–20 years. Namely, the expansion—and success—of independent league baseball has more and more fans attending independent league games in a way that suggests that affiliated minor league baseball is not fully meeting the needs of the baseball-as-entertainment market. Among other things, we'll be examining this independent league phenomenon with an eye towards using a proximity-based approach to studying the economic incentives that are prevalent in professional baseball.

At the same time that independent league teams are rising in popularity, all affiliated minor league baseball teams continue to be directly impacted by the business and personnel decisions of Major League Baseball teams. There is a uniqueness within professional baseball—apart from practically every other industry—that exists simply because Major League Baseball has been afforded the most generous protection by the US Supreme Court in the form of antitrust exemption. And as such, Major League Baseball is able to restrict entry of new teams into the market and increase consumer prices—the two most obvious outcomes of monopoly power when there are potential competitors in the market for high-quality baseball entertainment. It is this relationship that we want to examine using proximity as the lens through which we can structure our economic analysis. In other words, we want to examine more closely Major League Baseball's brand value that comes at least partly from the antitrust exemption status it has held for nearly a century by focusing exclusively on the proximity matters that are at the heart of so many decisions in professional baseball.

To my knowledge, no previous proximity-based approach to studying the economics of minor league baseball exists, making the major focus of this book a unique contribution to the sports economics literature. In studying minor league baseball by emphasizing the proximity issues that matter most in the structural development of professional baseball in America, it is my hope that this book will provide the reader with a better understanding of the economics behind minor league baseball. Throughout the book, I'll try to answer some of the questions that naturally arise from taking this kind of closer look at the business side of minor league baseball. For instance, why are more and more fans attending independent league baseball games? And why do affiliated minor league baseball teams have location restrictions placed on them by Major League Baseball? Are there better ways to align Major League Baseball teams with minor league affiliates? Proximity-based economic analysis provides us with a systematic way to approach finding an answer to each one of these questions.

This book is then, in one sense, a continuation of the growing body of work that sports economists are producing on minor league baseball. Similar techniques and similar models are used here as in the existing literature so that we can gauge the impact from key proximity factors in and around the minor league baseball arena on minor league baseball attendance. By using these similar techniques and models, we can make meaningful comparisons to the existing body of research.

To be clear, the key feature in this book that distinguishes the research here from the existing research on minor league baseball is the motivating story—proximity matters. To be more specific, in behaving as a legal monopoly Major League Baseball is able to impact affiliated minor league baseball in a unique and predictable way. This allows Major League Baseball's brand value to be quite high as they are the only producer of the highest caliber baseball in the world. Moreover, this brand value is kept high with the monopoly power they enjoy. It's this underlying framework of maintaining and enhancing the Major League Baseball brand value through controlling proximity issues that motivates much of the structure of minor league baseball today. Major League Baseball dictates so much of what goes on in minor league baseball, and much of it has not been studied by economists with a proximity-based approach in mind. For example, how and where minor league baseball teams are located, the level of play and the league minor league baseball teams play in, the size of their stadium, the composition of their player roster, and the Major League Baseball team they are affiliated with are all decisions almost entirely driven by Major League Baseball and not by the minor league team in affiliated baseball. These are all features of affiliated minor league baseball that potentially have impacts on attendance and subsequently on revenue and profit. But they are all also features of the business of professional baseball that are very much driven by proximity of Major League Baseball teams to minor league affiliates and by the proximity of those minor league baseball teams to other minor league teams within the same organization. In other words, as the business of affiliated minor league baseball is driven by the monopoly power enjoyed and employed by Major League Baseball, proximity between and to minor league baseball teams is a critical piece of the affiliated professional baseball business model.

However, independent league baseball operates under a different framework than affiliated minor league baseball, so all the decisions noted above are made by the independent minor league team apart from any overt influence of Major League Baseball. Independent league baseball teams are not restricted locationally, nor do they have stadium or roster requirements imposed on them by Major League Baseball. That is, independent league baseball teams are able to make decisions that are profit driven, without another organization besides their league administrators mandating what they can and cannot do. It's only when we keep in mind the influence of Major League Baseball on minor league baseball decisions that we get a chance to better understand the current state of minor league baseball and see how proximity-based decisions within professional baseball are driven so much by the antitrust exemption given to Major League Baseball. That Major League Baseball's antitrust exemption has a direct impact on minor league baseball makes professional baseball in the US unique, which makes our systematic study of professional baseball in this book unique as well.

Telling the story of minor league baseball while focusing on how proximity between baseball teams links minor league baseball and Major League Baseball has not been done yet in a systematic way using economic analysis. In fact, existing economic research has mostly left this corner of research unexplored—most economic research on minor league baseball touches on other subjects. There have been labor market studies that center on the development of player talent in the minor league baseball system (see Spurr and Barber 1994; Winfree and Molitor 2007; Burger and Walters 2009; Longley and Wong 2011). This research thread largely acknowledges the impact Major League Baseball has as a monopsonist over the labor market for professional baseball players. Still more work suggests that predicting the future value of a minor league baseball player to a Major League Baseball team is a difficult but potentially lucrative endeavor (see Lewis 2003; Bradbury 2007, 2011). Some research has also shown how Major League Baseball and affiliated minor league baseball can sometimes be regarded by baseball fans as substitutes (Gitter and Rhoads 2010). But the economic studies focused on minor league baseball really do not begin with the monopoly position of Major League Baseball setting the parameters for where the teams are located as a framework for examining the structural uniqueness of professional baseball—surprisingly little economic research has focused on the proximity issues that arise in professional baseball and how Major League Baseball has imposed its monopoly power in a way that potentially impacts the locational decisions (see Davis 2006, 2007; Roberts 2003). This is a critical part of minor league baseball, and it is this relationship that drives the proximity-based study of minor league baseball that we undertake in this book.

Major League Baseball's Antitrust Exemption

As America's pastime, baseball holds a unique place in this country's collective history. It's not just in how children once spent large portions of their summer leisure time—for decades, baseball was the sport of choice for many children on the sandlot and on the local ball field. But professional baseball games broadcast on the radio and increasingly on television grabbed the attention of a nation coming out of war and heading towards a new era of peace and prosperity. Baseball seemed to represent so much of what was great about this country at its greatest moment in history. Heroics on the baseball field, modern technology to deliver baseball games to the modern fan, and fun for the whole family all blended together through the mid-part of the American century to make baseball America's pastime. It was not entirely wrong to conclude that America's pastime was indeed the business of America.

But even while the game of baseball was emerging as America's pastime, the business of professional baseball was uniquely emerging from what Andrew Zimbalist (2003) calls a presumed antitrust exemption. In some ways, that development could be described as a reflection of typical business development in America. But in another very major way, the manner in which professional baseball developed was unique among industry in America. A closer look at how the business of professional baseball emerged provides a unique opportunity to observe business development in America, and specifically, how proximity to fans, other businesses, and franchise locations affects business decisions in America.

After facing competition from a rival professional baseball league and an ensuing legal case, Major League Baseball emerged from a Supreme Court ruling in 1922 with antitrust exemption. This ruling permitted Major League Baseball clubs to effectively be granted legal monopoly status. Note that antitrust legislation in the US is in place to prevent the dead weight loss that is expected to occur as a result of firms exercising monopoly power which comes in the form of restricting production and increasing prices consumers face. The fact that antitrust legislation exists in the US is at least partly a reflection of the fact that left unchecked, business owners in this country will try to turn their business into a monopoly so that they can enjoy the relatively large monopoly profits. In some way, then, Major League Baseball owners have achieved what practically all business owners want—legal monopoly status. It is this unique business structure throughout all of affiliated professional baseball that is the motivation for undertaking this proximity-based economic study of minor league baseball.

Minor League Baseball Structure

Let's begin by looking at what we mean to study in minor league baseball and why. First, we will refer to minor league baseball most generally as all the professional baseball leagues that are almost exclusively based in the US at levels below the highest professional level of baseball, that is, below Major League Baseball. While there are professional baseball leagues commonly associated with minor league baseball in many popular contexts—for example, the Mexican League and both the Dominican and Venezuela Summer Leagues—we will ignore those leagues in our studies in this book. Minor league baseball teams that are affiliated with Major League Baseball are considered to be in affiliated baseball, while those teams with no direct affiliation to Major League Baseball are independent. These two general distinctions, centered on affiliation status, will play a critical part in our study of minor league baseball and proximity.

Affiliated Baseball

Affiliated baseball is the term given to a set of professional baseball leagues that have a close affiliation with Major League Baseball. The Professional Baseball Agreement dictates the formal relationship between Major League Baseball and the National Association of Professional Baseball Leagues, or more commonly referenced as minor league baseball. Each baseball team that is an affiliated member of minor league baseball has a relationship with one Major League Baseball team that provides the player and coaching personnel for the affiliated minor league team. Rule 56 of the Major League Rules provides the details of the Player Development Contract that guides this business relationship between each minor league baseball team and its parent Major League Baseball team. For example, the Frederick Keys play in the Carolina League and are based in Frederick, Maryland, which is about 45 miles from Baltimore, Maryland. They are the Class A Advanced affiliate of the Baltimore Orioles, so their roster comprises players in the Orioles organization that are mostly at the early, but not necessarily the beginning, stages of their professional baseball career.

As players on the Keys develop more and more skill, they may move on to the Bowie Baysox, the Double-A affiliate of the Orioles. It's a decision that is made by Orioles management; the Keys organization really has nothing to do with when and where players are assigned. In all, there are six distinct levels of play in affiliated baseball, but we will be focusing on just the four highest of those levels in this book—Triple A, Double A, Class A Advanced, and Class A. We'll ignore the lowest two levels of affiliated baseball—Class A Short Season and Rookie—because, by most accounts, they are not significantly different in quality of play than college baseball and because they play a considerably shorter season of games. In other words, we want to look at professional baseball leagues where the quality of play is decidedly professional and not potentially perceived by fans as too close to amateur. Additionally, we want to examine the four highest levels of minor league baseball because they play a full season of games, which is the most similar to Major League Baseball and allows further comparisons between possible substitutes.

The relationship between a minor league baseball team and its Major League Baseball affiliate includes an expectation that in the process of the affiliated minor league team providing baseball-as-entertainment, the players and coaches will be developed so that they can have a chance to move to higher and higher levels of play. The goal is to develop the players and coaches to the point of being able to play and coach at the Major League Baseball level. To demonstrate this point, former players for the Keys include current Orioles players Manny Machado and Matt Wieters. Both of them were first-round draft picks by the Orioles and both of them are esteemed in Baltimore as being "homegrown" Orioles. And they have both had success at the Major League level, after developing and moving through the Orioles minor league system—both are Gold Glove Award winners and both have played in the All-Star Game.

In developing the link between Major League Baseball and affiliated minor league baseball, we first note that affiliated baseball teams are not in control of the baseball product on the field. In fact, they are responsible for every other element of the game apart from player and coach personnel. This includes the stadium, parking, concessions, marketing, and more. Clearly, there is a benefit from being directly connected to the most valuable brand in professional baseball—Major League Baseball. But each affiliated baseball team is potentially required to rely on elements of baseball-as-entertainment to drive revenue for the baseball team that are not field related because the minor league team may not win many games and may not have many top prospects. Additionally, the affiliated Major League Baseball team may not be winning or be a preferred choice of fans in that community. Winning matters some—not a lot—as my colleague Seth Gitter and I have found out (2010).

Independent League Baseball

Independent league baseball teams are not affiliated with any Major League Baseball team at all, suggesting that player and coach personnel decisions are made primarily with a profit incentive in mind. In this type of professional baseball business model, there are two likely reasons players and coaches are signed by an independent league team. First, player and coach signings could be made with the explicit intent to help the team win ball games. In this case and given budgetary constraints, independent league teams would seek out the best talent available for their roster with the hope of winning more ball games, attracting more fans, and therefore generating more revenue.

Seth Gitter and I previously determined that winning-affiliated minor league baseball teams only attract a small number of additional fans, but it may not be the case that the impact on independent league baseball teams would be the same. After all, these teams largely attract fans through a commitment by the teams to win games, and not simply to be a player development setting. The Atlantic League—one of the premier independent baseball leagues in North America—boasts about this feature on their league website: "Atlantic League clubs pay their players to win baseball games, not be apprentices as in the developmental levels."[4] But even as the Atlantic League is quick to put distance between themselves and an unwanted element of affiliated minor league baseball—the inability to control the product on the field—they are quick to also point out that their players are "Major League ready" and that "over 600 Atlantic League players have been signed by Major League clubs."[5] Thus, the Atlantic League is demonstrating the delicate balance of steering clear of the potentially undesirable aspect of affiliated minor league baseball—a perception of not always playing to win—while at the same

[4] Accessed http://atlanticleague.com/about.html on October 23, 2014.

[5] Accessed http://atlanticleague.com/about.html on October 23, 2014.

time highlighting the link to Major League Baseball, which is the most valuable brand in professional baseball.

Alternatively, independent league teams can sign players and coaches for the primary purpose of bringing fans to the stadium, regardless of the talent of the player or coach in question or their ability to help the team win games. Sometimes these players are former Major League Baseball players that still have a chance to attract fans to the ballpark that want to watch them play. In these types of situations, winning is not what always matters; bringing fans to the stadium and creating a buzz is what is primary in these player signings.

This certainly seems to have been the case in 2012 when the Sugar Land Skeeters, in their first year of existence in the Atlantic League, signed former Cy Young Award winner Roger Clemens to pitch in two home games. The second game Clemens started attracted 8,597 fans to Constellation Field in Sugar Land, Texas, a stadium with a capacity of 7,500. That game set the highest attendance mark of the season for the Skeeters, a season in which they sold out nearly every one of their home games in their inaugural season. While Clemens pitched very well for the Skeeters, it is likely that his signing was more a publicity opportunity for the Skeeters to attract more fans towards the end of a season with slim playoff possibilities. And it seems to have worked.[6]

For this reason, or for any number of other legitimate reasons, independent league baseball offers former Major League Baseball players an opportunity to keep playing professional baseball when affiliated professional baseball is no longer interested in them. And, as in the case of Roger Clemens and the Sugar Land Skeeters, this can bring fans to the stadium. But independent league baseball offers a unique opportunity for us as we take a proximity-based approach to the economics of minor league baseball. Namely, independent league baseball teams are not restricted from locating too close to other professional baseball teams in their own league or in other leagues. Constellation Field, where the Sugar Land Skeeters play their home games, is in Fort Bend County, Texas, and is less than 20 miles away from Minute Maid Park, where Major League Baseball's Houston Astros play their home games.

Rule 52 of the Major League Rules provides clear rules on where both Major League Baseball teams and affiliated minor league baseball teams are permitted to locate. The Skeeters—not being part of the Professional Baseball Agreement—are free to locate anywhere their ownership desires. And in fact, the Skeeters play their home games in the home territory of the Houston Astros as designated in Attachment 52 of the Major League Rules. The closest affiliated minor league baseball team to the Houston Astros is the Round Rock Express, located nearly 150 miles from Minute Maid Park. And the Round Rock Express are not located in the home territory of the Houston Astros.

---

[6] Before Roger Clemens pitched for the Skeeters, a federal jury in the summer of 2012 found him not guilty of lying to Congress in his 2008 testimony regarding his alleged use of performance-enhancing drugs. Pitching for the Skeeters was perhaps as beneficial to Clemens in confirming the jury's finding as it was for the Skeeters in bringing more fans to the ballpark.

This example of an independent league baseball team locating rather close to an established Major League Baseball team is not unique. The Camden Riversharks of the Atlantic League, another independent league baseball team in the same league as the Sugar Land Skeeters, is located within the home territory of the Philadelphia Phillies. There are even more examples of independent league baseball teams located within the home territories of Major League Baseball teams and affiliated minor league baseball teams. Because independent league baseball teams have no explicit locational restrictions placed on them, we can assume that team owners and league officials have every incentive to place each team in an optimal location to maximize profit for the team and the league. Thus, our casual observation that profit-driven independent league baseball teams are located and succeed in areas that are largely off limits to affiliated minor league baseball teams suggests that Major League Baseball is largely using the friendly Supreme Court ruling from 1922 to restrict competing teams from locating too close to existing teams. This is rather strong observational evidence suggesting that proximity matters in professional baseball and points to the direction the research in this book will be heading.

Where Are We Heading?

The discussion above raises an important and relevant question concerning all minor league baseball teams. In particular, does proximity to other professional baseball teams matter for a typical minor league baseball team? From at least a couple of different perspectives, we aim to address that question in this book.

In the next chapter, I begin with a regression analysis that examines the effect proximity has on minor league baseball attendance. The economics literature so far has focused on attendance for minor league baseball teams as the primary means of testing the impact of policy on the business of minor league baseball. I continue in that line of research while incorporating independent league baseball into the analysis. The results suggest that loosening restrictions on where minor league baseball teams are permitted to locate could lead to higher attendance across all minor league baseball stadiums.

Chapters 3, 4, and 5 together offer a unique perspective on how proximity matters for Major League Baseball teams seeking to improve player development opportunities. These chapters form the core of the book. In Chapter 3, I suggest that a Major League Baseball team's proximity to its minor league affiliate can significantly affect the player development process. In Chapter 4, I introduce the concept of a Pareto efficient allocation mechanism to the affiliate shuffle which allows me to provide a metric by which the aggregate distance between all Major League Baseball teams and their minor league affiliates at each level can be assessed. Finally, in Chapter 5, I suggest making some switches to the current allocation of affiliates that would be Pareto improvements to the current setting. If being closer to a minor league affiliate can lead to enhancements in player development, policy makers in

Major League Baseball can potentially provide the setting to allow certain affiliation switches to occur in order to best develop players at the minor league level. Chapter 6 offers some possible directions to take the conclusions found in this book further. We move on now to developing the regression model in Chapter 2.

Chapter 2
Proximity's Impact on Minor League Baseball Attendance

As we noted in Chap. 1 and as many other researchers have carefully documented, Major League Baseball's antitrust exemption has led to certain regulations meant to favor Major League Baseball team owners with less regard for the owners of minor league baseball teams.[1] Namely, the restriction on Major League Baseball teams and affiliated minor league baseball teams from building a home baseball stadium too close to an existing Major League Baseball stadium is largely designed to maintain monopoly power for the Major League team already established within that locality. Keeping potential substitute goods away tends to decrease the number of fans that are considering attending a competing on-the-field product. Additionally, the restriction allows Major League teams to charge higher ticket prices in the absence of competing substitute professional baseball games. Already, there is evidence that attending other Major League Baseball games or minor league baseball games can serve as a substitute for fans of Major League Baseball games within moderate driving distance to stadiums where the games are played (Gitter and Rhoads 2010 and Winfree et al. 2004).

The regulations we focus on here and that serve as the motivation for our analysis throughout the book involve proximity of minor league baseball teams to other affiliated professional baseball teams. The term affiliated professional baseball teams can include both Major League Baseball teams and minor league baseball teams that are affiliated, through a Professional Development Contract, with a Major League Baseball team. A proximity-based approach to examining the economics of minor league baseball allows us to focus on the regulations set by Major League Baseball that are largely intended to protect the monopoly rents enjoyed by

[1] See either of Andrew Zimbalist's books on the business of baseball to get a good sense of how antitrust exemption for Major League Baseball came about and what it means for the professional baseball industry in America. Two of his books are Baseball and Billions: A probing look inside the big business of our national pastime (1992) and May the Best Team Win: Baseball Economics and Public Policy (2003).

© Springer Science+Business Media New York 2015

T.A. Rhoads, *The Call Up to the Majors*, Sports Economics, Management and Policy 7, DOI 10.1007/978-1-4614-8924-5_2

Major League Baseball teams but additionally end up having an impact on the business of minor league baseball teams.

By structuring regulations to limit the locational decisions of minor league baseball teams, Major League Baseball essentially controls the geographic distribution of all professional baseball teams in affiliated baseball. This includes all 30 Major League teams and all of their affiliated minor league teams at every level of play. We can expect that owners of Major League Baseball teams and minor league baseball teams will treat proximity between affiliated professional baseball teams differently. This difference in perspective on the business impact of proximity frames the analysis throughout this book, and we focus on proximity impacts on minor league baseball teams in this chapter. The remainder of the book, and the bulk of our analysis, will address proximity concerns from the perspective of Major League Baseball teams.

Our examination of the locational choices of minor league baseball will explore in detail how the decisions made by Major League Baseball within the scope of the Major League Rules can impact the business of minor league baseball. We pay close attention to attendance for minor league baseball teams because the viability of a minor league baseball team relies largely on bringing fans to the game. Unlike Major League Baseball, minor league baseball teams generate no major revenue streams coming from national and regional television contracts. This means that minor league baseball revenue is almost exclusively generated from ticket sales, advertising and promotions, food and beverage concessions, and merchandise (Solomon 2012). And because of the substitutability of live professional baseball games at the ballpark, the revenue stream for a minor league baseball team can be impacted negatively by the proximity of the team to other minor league and Major League teams. Compared to the owners of Major League Baseball teams, the owners of minor league baseball teams are therefore much more dependent on fans attending the games for their business operations to be successful.

With a focus on attendance at minor league games, proximity becomes one of the most important factors impacting the business of minor league baseball. There is an optimal distance away from other minor league baseball stadiums as well as an optimal distance from a Major League Baseball stadium that can lead to maximum stadium revenues for the minor league ownership. Without easy access to the profit and loss statements for privately owned professional baseball teams, it is not possible to test the effect of proximity on the bottom line of a minor league baseball team. Instead, we will examine the effect of proximity on average attendance at minor league baseball games with the understanding that greater average attendance is likely to be strongly correlated with a larger revenue stream. At the minor league level greater attendance is preferred, all else equal, due to the very limited revenue stream from broadcasting these games on television, radio, and the Internet. And because close proximity to other professional baseball teams' home stadiums can potentially take fans away, minor league baseball teams are potentially quite dependent on being located an optimal distance from other baseball stadiums.

Major League Rule 52

Rule 52 of the Major League Rules precisely lays out the territorial rights for both Major League and for minor league baseball teams. Major League Baseball's antitrust exemption provides the opportunity to design a business setting meant to protect Major League Baseball teams as much as possible from competition. Preventing other professional baseball teams from establishing a home territory and building a stadium that could potentially take fans away are direct results of the antitrust exemption. And it can be a very effective tool that benefits both Major League and minor league baseball teams.

The general stipulation in Rule 52 is that affiliated professional baseball teams may not play their home games in a stadium that is closer than 15 miles from the boundaries of the home territory of any other affiliated baseball team. While there are certain exceptions, this rule is designed to limit the live professional baseball entertainment opportunities for fans in any locality with an already established affiliated baseball team. This gives pricing power to the established team while simultaneously directing potential fans to the team.

We will examine the impact of distance between stadiums on attendance while holding certain other variables constant. This allows us to provide some insight into this unique setting that characterizes professional affiliated baseball. But before we get a chance to discuss that model, we have to recognize that independent league baseball can give us an equally unique opportunity to determine how distance between stadiums impacts attendance. Because independent league baseball operates in a setting without an antitrust exemption dictating the rules and structure of the league, we can begin to identify how professional baseball teams at the level just below Major League Baseball organize and position themselves geographically. In other words, independent league baseball offers a kind of natural experiment in how professional baseball teams determine where to locate when there is no larger organization providing the rules of organization.

Independent league baseball has been recognized as a viable and emerging substitute to affiliated professional baseball for at least a decade (Zimbalist 2003) and continues to grow. The Atlantic League of Professional Baseball formed in 1998 and bills itself as "the only professional baseball league in an active expansion mode."[2] And because independent league baseball is not affiliated with Major League Baseball, it provides a setting that is not influenced directly by certain Major League Rules—like Rule 52—that can be seen as protecting the monopoly power of current Major League Baseball teams. Identifying key features of the way independent leagues geographically organize themselves can help us to highlight how distance to other stadiums—within the same league and within affiliated baseball—and the geographic density of minor leagues can affect attendance at professional baseball games. We examine these features next.

[2] The Atlantic League is considering expanding from 8 to 12 teams within the next few years, according to their website, http://atlanticleague.com/about.html. Accessed on August 11, 2014.

Background

Proximity to other baseball stadiums can impact attendance at minor league baseball games. Some elements of this proximity must be highlighted before we determine its effect on attendance. Minor league baseball games are live entertainment that are typically aimed at young families and compete with other entertainment options like movies and concerts (Solomon 2012). The Atlantic League notes on its website that its baseball is a "fun and affordable family entertainment experience for fans of ALL ages."[3] Minor league baseball president and CEO Pat O'Connor describes minor league baseball as having "the thrills of a theme park, the emotions of a good movie, the element of surprise at a concert and the cuisine of your favorite restaurant."[4]

Families have a limited budget for entertainment options such as movies, concerts, restaurants, and live sporting events. The fact that minor league marketing efforts note these features draws attention to the competitive nature of the entertainment market, of which Major League Baseball is also a part but has branded itself as something different as the premier brand of professional baseball in the world. Further, these features point to the value to owners of Major League Baseball teams—and to a lesser degree also to owners of minor league baseball teams—from placing geographic restrictions within the Major League Rules on where stadiums are allowed to be built in affiliated baseball. In effect, independent league baseball and affiliated minor league baseball market themselves in a very similar fashion while being subject to market pressures from similar substitute goods. This fact alone suggests a unique opportunity to examine how the antitrust exemption that allows Major League Baseball to place geographical constraints on where affiliated baseball stadiums are located compares to the decisions within independent league baseball, where there are no locational restrictions stemming from antitrust exemption status.

The locational features of minor league baseball games—both affiliated and independent—necessarily imply that fans must be in close proximity to the stadium to enjoy the game. Although more and more minor league baseball games are being broadcast on the Internet through outlets such as milb.tv and the websites for independent league teams, the quality of these broadcasts cannot compete with Major League Baseball broadcasts on any kind of media device. As a result, minor league baseball games are almost exclusively consumed by a paying fan at the stadium as a live event. This differs from Major League Baseball, which can attract fans through local and regional television broadcasts in addition to those that purchase a ticket to attend a game at the stadium.

[3] http://atlanticleague.com/about.html. Accessed on August 11, 2014.

[4] O'Connor wrote these things in an open letter to Dr. Mark Emmert, president of the National Collegiate Athletic Association, in June 2014. Emmert had recently testified in an antitrust lawsuit against the NCAA that "U.S. minor league sports aren't very successful either for fan support or for the fan experience." O'Connor's comments were meant to counter Emmert's contention that it would be a mistake to turn college sports into something similar to minor league sports.

Local, regional, and national television broadcast rights for Major League Baseball teams can be quite lucrative and provide a large portion of revenue for the team. These television revenues can now be measured in the billions of dollars, placing Major League Baseball in a completely different entertainment option than minor league baseball. Thus, Major League Baseball and minor league baseball can really only be considered substitutes for the baseball fan attending a game at the stadium. And while there are other entertainment options to compete with Major League Baseball games on television, regional sports networks that broadcast Major League Baseball games have some of the highest rated programming in local markets in the US. In many markets in the US, prime time television ratings are dominated by Major League Baseball games broadcast on regional sports channels.[5] This all suggests the value of Major League Baseball as a brand is quite high, and minor league baseball executives working in both affiliated and independent league baseball do their best to link their product to it.

Attendance at Professional Baseball Games

All of the discussion in the previous section about baseball as entertainment points to the following—minor league baseball is an entertainment option for fans who desire to attend a baseball game in person at the stadium. Major League Baseball stadiums and other minor league baseball stadiums that are nearby can serve as substitutes for the marginal minor league baseball fan. A minor league baseball fan at the margin is not meant to be a simple reference to the fan's level of allegiance to the team. Instead, the marginal fan is described as a fan that makes a decision to attend a game based on a number of different factors that can be measured. In fact, some of these factors are examined in more detail throughout the remainder of this chapter. And minor league baseball fans can be characterized as being concerned with affordable entertainment that can compete with movies, concerts, and restaurants. As such, we can identify some characteristics of minor league baseball teams that follow directly from our current discussion about what leads to fans attending minor league baseball games. But even more, the characteristics that we identify are also the same as what are typically included in the attendance models in the sports economics literature.

---

[5] Nearly half (12 out of 29) of the Major League Baseball teams based in the US held the top spot in prime time television ratings in the summer of 2014. http://www.forbes.com/sites/maurybrown/2014/08/05/mlb-telecasts-on-regional-sports-networks-dominate-prime-time-television/ Accessed on August 11, 2014.

The Data

The variable I am most concerned about describing in my analysis is average attendance at minor league baseball games. The number of fans that attend a minor league baseball game is perhaps the most important factor in determining success or failure of the minor league team as a business entity. Not only will more fans bring in more ticket revenue, but more fans also allow for more concessions and merchandise sales and increase advertising revenue. Business success for a minor league baseball team is not assured as there are many substitute entertainment options available to possible paying fans. In fact, there are plenty of examples of minor league baseball teams—especially independent league teams—that have folded for failing to maintain a large enough revenue stream. Many of these teams that folded had problems attracting fans to the stadium and subsequently did not have a strong enough revenue stream to remain a viable business.

One somewhat recent example of an independent league team folding is the Coastal Bend Aviators from the American Association. The Aviators folded in 2007 and one of the primary reasons for the team's demise was the lackluster ticket sales. Total attendance for each of the final three seasons the Aviators were in Robstown, Texas, was well below 100,000, with average attendance well under 2,000 fans per game. Robstown is only about 20 miles from Corpus Christi, Texas, where the Hooks began playing in the Double A-level Texas League in 2005. The Hooks are the Double A affiliate of the Houston Astros which, at 183 miles away, also happens to be the closest Major League Baseball team to Corpus Christi. Total attendance for the Hooks was about 500,000 in each of their first three seasons at Whataburger Field, and average attendance was about 7,200. As shown in Table 2.1 below, the first three seasons of existence for the Hooks and the last three seasons of existence for the Aviators could not show a more pronounced difference in attendance for two teams playing at somewhat similar levels of professional baseball and located relatively close to each other.

The example given above is especially pronounced given that the Aviators had built their stadium in 2003 and the Hooks had their stadium built in 2005. In fact, it is not difficult to make generalizations from this one example. First, location compared to other baseball stadiums matters. The Aviators were only playing games about 20 miles away from the Hooks in a metropolitan area with a population of around 500,000. Second, age of the stadium matters, with new minor league stadiums typically drawing significantly more fans (see Gitter and Rhoads 2014).

Table 2.1 Attendance for Aviators and Hooks baseball teams

	2004	2005	2006	2007
Coastal Bend Aviators				
Total	103,049	79,826	85,862	58,715
Average	2,146	1,698	1,788	1,276
Corpus Christi Hooks				
Total	No games played	505,189	506,398	479,289
Average		7,216	7,234	7,048

While still being relatively new, the Aviators home stadium was no longer the newest minor league baseball stadium in the metropolitan area once the Hooks began playing home games in Corpus Christi. Finally, being affiliated with Major League Baseball directly through a player development contract is likely to provide lucrative opportunities for additional revenue through higher ticket sales.

Each of these elements, and more, can be included in a model to describe average attendance. It is critical when building a model like this to include data describing many of the factors that are expected to influence average attendance. It should not be surprising that prior research on minor league baseball attendance has been helpful in building this model. In this section, I provide some detail about the data that I used to build this model.

I collected data for all full-season affiliated minor league teams from 2006 to 2013. This includes Class A, Class A Advanced, Double A, and Triple A. I also collected data over the same time period from the teams in the four major independent leagues of professional baseball. These leagues include the American Association, the Atlantic League, the Can-Am League, and the Frontier League. All of the attendance, stadium age, and win-loss data for these teams were collected from the annual Baseball America Directory for each of the years in the data sample.

Zip codes for each of the stadiums of the teams in this data set were collected from the Baseball America Directory and then entered into the zip code distance calculator on the website www.zip-codes.com. I used the baseball travel guide on the website www.baseball-reference.com/travel to determine the number of minor league teams within the same league that are within 100 miles of each team in the data set. This was done for both affiliated and independent minor league teams. In earlier research, Seth Gitter and I defined a local team as being within 100 miles of a fan (2010), so I am staying consistent with that definition. While admittedly not a simple thing to do, most people can potentially travel to attend a baseball game any day of the week, even after work, provided they live within 100 miles of a stadium. At a minimum, the 100-mile delineation provides a focal point which almost all fans would agree serves as a maximum one-way distance to travel to see a game.

Additionally, I used the baseball travel guide to determine the closest affiliated Major League and minor league baseball teams to each of the teams in my data set. In collecting data on the distance to the closest affiliated baseball teams at the Major League and minor league levels and the geographic dispersion of teams within the minor league, substitute affiliated professional baseball games are recognized as important elements affecting attendance. Primarily because the Major League Baseball brand is valuable as the premier professional baseball league in the world, proximity to the closest Major League Baseball team and affiliated minor league team attempts to capture this element affecting attendance. Further, the restrictions placed on affiliated minor league baseball teams in Major League Rule 52 to playing home games a certain minimum distance from other affiliated minor league teams and Major League Baseball teams suggest that proximity to affiliated professional baseball stadiums could impact attendance.

Close proximity to affiliated baseball stadiums is expected to affect attendance, but the density of teams within the league could matter as well. This is because attendance for a minor league baseball team is not just a function of home fans' preferences. Fans of other teams in the same league may also have a preference to watch their team at an away stadium. Traveling to another team's stadium to attend a game as a fan of the away team can be a signal of the strength of the fan's preferences. But it can also be a function of ticket price and availability and stadium quality for the fan's home team. In either case, closer proximity to an away stadium within the same league could lead to higher attendance as more possible people are potentially willing and able to purchase a ticket to the game.

A recent Major League Baseball example of proximity to the away baseball stadium helps to illustrate this point further. The Washington Nationals attracted national media attention in 2012 for their "Take Back the Park" campaign that was intended to minimize the number of Philadelphia Phillies fans that would make the trip to Nationals Park in Washington, DC to watch their Phillies play. An A-Hed article in The Wall Street Journal from May 2012 provides insight into why away fans may consider traveling to an away stadium to see their team play.[6] At the time, Phillies tickets were very difficult to come by and subsequently they were expensive to purchase for home games at Citizens Bank Park—the Phillies had sold out well over 200 straight games (about three straight seasons of games). Phillies fans were finding the relatively short trip south on Interstate-95 a viable option to attend a Phillies game. While minor league games are rarely ever sold out (except for the famous example of the Dayton Dragons with the record for consecutive sellouts for a North American professional sports team), the experience of Phillies fans taking a road trip to a stadium 125 miles from their own home baseball park illustrates a key factor in what affects attendance.

Proximity to the away ballpark makes it more likely that attendance at any given minor league baseball game could be higher because the away fans may take the trip to attend the game provided the game is close enough. Including a variable that measures the number of teams within 100 miles and are within the same league for every team in the data set gives an opportunity to measure the impact of how away fans may impact attendance. More teams in the same minor league with a tighter geographic density could also lead to lower ticket prices if minor league games are perceived to be substitute goods. But more teams in the same geographic area could lead to increased pressure for a limited number of tickets with the increased competition from additional fans. This could end up driving up the ticket price, which may lead to fewer home fan ticket sales. Unfortunately, ticket price data were not available for independent league teams for all of the years in the data set, so they are not included in the model. But it is expected that ticket prices may be picked up in the random effects model, and this point will be discussed later in the discussion of the results.

I previously examined attendance for minor league baseball from 1992 until 2006 in a number of different studies with my colleague Seth Gitter (Gitter and Rhoads 2010, 2011, 2014). The analysis here picks up in the same year where the prior research left off and offers a good opportunity for a comparison of the results.

[6] "For D.C. Baseball Team, Deluge of Phillies Fans Is National Disgrace" by Brad Reagan, The Wall Street Journal, A1, May 2, 2012.

Specifically, in estimating the value of the coefficients of the variables included in the model, I can check them against the results in the previous research to be sure that the model is most likely built properly and gives reasonable results. It will become clear that the results in this analysis are comparable to those from earlier studies.

Descriptive statistics are included in Table 2.2 below. Again, the intention with the analysis here is to determine if there are some uniquely different ways that independent baseball leagues structure themselves compared to affiliated minor league baseball. The absence of rules from an organization maintaining monopoly rents derived from antitrust exemption suggests a type of league structure for independent league baseball that is more dependent on the benefits of being optimally located in comparison to other teams, but for which maintaining or keeping monopoly power

Table 2.2 Descriptive statistics

	Mean	St. Dev.	Min.	Max.
Average attendance				
Triple A	6,640	1,729	1,915	10,257
Double A	4,466	1,429	1,404	8,413
Class A Advanced	2,254	1,085	430	4,914
Class A	3,610	1,805	835	8,624
Independent league	2,980	1,311	453	6,786
Closest MLB team, in miles				
Triple A	151.19	89.44	26	371
Double A	145.71	89.25	14	347
Class A Advanced	90.10	78.31	17	316
Class A	127.52	68.05	16	264
Independent league	73.25	82.85	3	346
Closest MiLB team, in miles				
Triple A	84.44	63.86	22	283
Double A	80.66	52.55	24	273
Class A Advanced	27.49	24.96	1	89
Class A	59.49	22.35	20	125
Independent league	66.31	56.79	9	223
Rival teams within 100 miles				
Triple A	0.20	0.48	0	2
Double A	0.75	0.80	0	3
Class A Advanced	2.94	1.95	0	7
Class A	1.69	1.58	0	6
Independent league	1.69	1.54	0	10
Stadium age, in years				
Triple A	18.11	17.29	0	84
Double A	14.07	12.69	0	74
Class A Advanced	30.02	24.27	0	90
Class A	22.13	23.87	0	82
Independent league	21.98	28.93	0	107

is not explicitly the goal. It must be noted that while Major League Baseball's exercising monopoly power flows from being granted antitrust exemption by the US Supreme Court, it is quite possible that independent league baseball may be structured in a similar fashion. The models developed here will therefore help to determine whether or not antitrust exemption may have led to certain locational decisions by Major League Baseball owners for determining where Major League and affiliated minor league teams should be based.

Before we develop the conditional average attendance model that will allow us to get a better sense of how minor league baseball leagues handle proximity to other baseball stadiums, we will use *t*-tests to give unconditional analysis of proximity. There are three variables that we will focus on in this unconditional analysis. MLBdist describes the direct line distance, in miles, from the minor league team to the closest Major League Baseball team. MiLBdist describes the direct line distance, in miles, between the minor league team and the nearest affiliated minor league baseball team. This includes all levels of full-season and short-season affiliated minor league baseball and helps estimate the value of the Major League Baseball brand value. RIVALS is a measure of the number of teams within 100 miles and in the same minor league as the minor league team in the data set. This variable helps to estimate the value of league rivalries and the effect of density of teams in a close geographic area.

Within-League Observations

The first observation to make is that among independent league baseball teams, the mean distance to the closest Major League Baseball team and the mean distance to the closest affiliated minor league baseball team at any level appear to be the same. Table 2.3 below includes the mean values for MLBdist, MiLBdist, and RIVALS for independent league and affiliated minor league baseball teams for the year 2013. A paired sample *t*-test of the values of MLBdist and MiLBdist for independent league teams ($t = -0.0051$) is conducted. Using this data set that includes 39 independent league baseball teams in operation in 2013, we cannot reject the null hypothesis that the distance from an independent league baseball team to either the closest Major League Baseball team or the closest affiliated minor league baseball team is the same. The mean value for both MLBdist and MiLBdist is 104. The unconditional analysis provided by the paired sample *t*-test suggests that independent league teams treat proximity to Major League Baseball teams and affiliated minor league baseball teams in a similar manner. It is impossible to determine the

Table 2.3 Mean values for MLBdist, MiLBdist, and RIVALS for 2013

	Triple A	Double A	Class A Advanced	Class A	Independent league
MLBdist	149.00	147.67	88.53	128.60	103.72
MiLBdist	84.73	79.43	26.00	59.40	103.80
RIVALS	0.20	0.80	2.97	1.67	1.51

reason for this equal distance to the closest team in affiliated baseball using this unconditional analysis, but it is notable that affiliated minor league baseball teams exhibit a different result when running a paired sample *t*-test of MLBdist and MiLBdist for each level of full-season affiliated minor league baseball.

The paired sample *t*-tests of MLBdist and MiLBdist for Class A ($t=5.19$), Class A Advanced ($t=4.92$), Double A ($t=4.86$), and Triple A ($t=3.54$) allow us to reject the null hypotheses that the values of MLBdist and MiLBdist are the same at every level of affiliated minor league baseball. In fact, at each level of affiliated baseball the mean distance to the closest minor league baseball team is less than the mean distance to the closest Major League Baseball team. The geographic reality of minor league baseball is that the teams are usually arranged within a minor league on a regional level more than at the Major League level. This will naturally lead to a setting where these teams are closer to each other than to Major League teams. Note that the Class A Advanced level of baseball is the only level of affiliated baseball for which the mean value of MLBdist is less than 100 miles.

Across-League Observations

We turn our attention now to comparing the mean values of MLBdist, MiLBdist, and RIVALS for each level of affiliated baseball to the same variables in independent league baseball. That is, we will shift attention away from comparing the sample means within levels to comparing them across levels of baseball. We will restrict our focus to comparing the variables of interest at each level of affiliated baseball to those same variables for independent league baseball. In this way, we can begin to assess whether or not any significant difference exists between the way affiliated and independent league baseball teams are geographically organized.

Table 2.4 below shows the results for each of the *t*-tests performed at each level of affiliated minor league baseball. The *t*-tests compare the sample mean at each level of affiliated minor league baseball for each of the MLBdist, MiLBdist, and RIVALS variables to independent league baseball. The results suggest that independent baseball appears to be structured in a way that is not exactly like any one level of affiliated minor league baseball, but does seem to have the most similarity with Class A-level baseball.

Starting with the variable MLBdist, *t*-tests show that independent league baseball appears to be similar to both Class A ($t=-1.11$) and Class A Advanced ($t=0.65$).

Table 2.4 Values for *t*-tests comparing affiliated minor league baseball sample means to independent league baseball sample means for 2013

	Triple A	Double A	Class A Advanced	Class A
MLBdist	−1.81	−1.76	0.65	−1.11
MiLBdist	0.89	1.20	4.24	2.42
RIVALS	4.08	2.08	−3.02	−0.36

That is, we cannot reject the null hypothesis that the sample mean distance between a Class A or Class A Advanced minor league baseball team and the nearest Major League Baseball team is the same as the sample mean distance between independent league baseball teams and the nearest Major League Baseball team. We can assume that affiliated minor league teams will be located further from Major League Baseball teams because of Rule 52 in the Major League Rules. Using this assumption, the data also suggest that we can reject the null hypothesis that Double A ($t=-1.76$) and Triple A ($t=-1.81$) level minor league baseball teams are located the same distance from Major League stadiums as independent league teams.[7] While these t-tests are unconditional, the results point to the possibility that when compared to independent league baseball teams, Double A and Triple A minor league teams may have more distance between themselves and Major League Baseball teams because the quality of baseball is relatively high.

Because Major League owners ultimately permit where the Double A and Triple A teams are located, there may be a concern that the two highest levels of full-season affiliated minor league baseball could serve as a viable alternative to Major League Baseball for those fans that respond to the presence of better quality baseball. At the same time, we could make a story that since the quality of play at the two lowest levels of full-season minor league baseball is quite a bit below the Major League level, there is not as much of a concern for Major League owners that fans of high-quality baseball will potentially attend a Class A- or Class A Advanced-level game instead of a Major League game. This analysis would also be consistent with assigning the lower levels of full-season affiliated minor league baseball as the preferred levels for rehabilitation assignments for Major League players.[8] Closer proximity to the affiliated Class A- or Class A Advanced-level team will not draw as many fans away from the Major League team based on the quality of baseball, compared to Double A or Triple A. But we must keep in mind that because this is all based on unconditional analysis, nothing more can be gleaned from the data. While these initial observations and stories seem reasonable, it is not possible to attach as much significance to them given the type of analysis.

The next variable to examine is MiLBdist, which measures the direct line distance from each minor league team in the data set to the nearest affiliated minor league baseball team, regardless of level. This includes short season and rookie league affiliated minor league baseball. Sometimes a top prospect first lands in professional baseball at the short season or rookie league minor league level. Fans are often drawn to attend those games in which the newest prospects appear, so the potential for minor league teams to draw other fans can occur at any level of affiliated baseball.

[7] If we do not assume greater distance from a Major League team to either a Double A or Triple A team, we can still reject the null hypothesis that the mean distance to the closest Major League Baseball team is the same for Double A , Triple A, and independent league baseball teams. We must use the more generous 10 % significance level and a two-tail test, however.

[8] Analyzing how Major League rehab assignments are made—to what level and for how long—seems like an area of research that is ready to examine using proximity-based analysis.

The mean direct line distance between independent league baseball teams and the nearest affiliated minor league baseball team appears to be similar to the Double A ($t = 1.20$) and Triple A ($t = 0.89$) level. That is, we cannot reject the null hypothesis that the mean direct line distance from independent league, Double A, or Triple A baseball teams to the nearest affiliated minor league team is the same. Alternatively, t-tests show this mean distance to be different when comparing independent leagues to Class A ($t = 2.42$) or Class A Advanced ($t = 4.24$) leagues. We reject the null hypothesis that the mean direct line distance from independent league, Class A-, or Class A Advanced-level baseball teams is the same.

With no restrictions coming from Major League Baseball on where to locate, independent league team owners presumably have an incentive to locate an optimal distance from other professional baseball teams. Of course there are many constraints that can restrict where an independent league baseball team locates. These constraints include proximity to other existing teams within the league, location of a city with favorable demographics that is able to host the team, and political climate—including the tax laws—in which the new team and a newly constructed stadium would begin operating. We can assume that the optimal direct line distance would be meant to provide the best opportunity to avoid competing with other professional baseball teams playing their home games in relatively close geographic proximity. The data so far seems to suggest that Double A- and Triple A-level minor league baseball teams are situated in geographic proximity to the closest minor league team that is similar to the way independent league baseball is arranged. While this is only unconditional analysis, the evidence is consistent with Double A and Triple A baseball teams wanting to avoid competition from other minor league baseball teams.

At the same time, the data suggest that Class A- and Class A Advanced-level baseball teams locate in a manner that is unlike independent league baseball teams when it comes to proximity to other minor league teams. On average, Class A and Class A Advanced teams are closer to the nearest affiliated minor league baseball team than independent league teams are located to their closest affiliated minor league team. While this is only unconditional analysis, the data suggest that Class A- and Class A Advanced-level minor league baseball teams are not geographically placed in such a way that could optimize the number of fans attending games and the revenue generated at the ballpark during those games. Perhaps more important, this result also suggests that the Major League Baseball brand that is attached to all levels of affiliated minor league baseball may be worth enough to offset the possible close proximity effects at the lower levels of affiliated minor league baseball. This is an important element to feature in a model describing average attendance at minor league baseball games and will be included in a discussion of the results of the conditional model in the next section.

The unconditional analysis of the MLBdist and MiLBdist variables together suggests that independent league baseball teams position themselves a similar distance from affiliated minor league baseball teams as do Double A- and Triple A-level teams and from Major League Baseball teams as do Class A- and Class A Advanced-level teams. Some observations arise. First, independent league baseball must provide an entertainment package similar to affiliated minor league baseball without the Major League Baseball brand attached to it. While there is no shortage of references to players having already played or are now ready to play at the highest level of professional baseball, independent league baseball does not have the same brand recognition as does affiliated minor league baseball. This requires strategic location choices for independent league baseball teams so that nuanced marketing opportunities can target baseball fans that may not be influenced as much by the Major League Baseball brand. This may be more likely for areas that are further from a Major League Baseball team or are in the same market as multiple Major League Baseball teams so that shared loyalty is not unusual.

Second, independent league baseball appears to balance the entertainment elements of the game day experience with the quality of the baseball game itself. Along with independent league baseball, in some regard the quality of Double A- and Triple A-level baseball is of a high enough caliber that fans could loosely put them in a class of baseball entertainment along with Major League Baseball and not with Class A- or Class A Advanced-level baseball. Many of the players on an independent league team or on a Double A- or Triple A-level team are one step away from Major League Baseball. At the Class A or Class A Advanced level of minor league baseball, many of the players are at least two steps away from Major League Baseball. Major League Baseball has earned the distinction of being the highest quality of professional baseball in the world, for which there is no substitute for any fan desiring to attend a game exhibiting the highest level of play. As such, proximity to a Major League Baseball team must be a major consideration for professional baseball teams at the level just below Major League Baseball. John Feinstein, in his book *Where Nobody Knows Your Name*, notes how Gwinnett Braves manager Dave Brundage is aware of the difficulty of attracting fans to a Triple A-level team located about 30 miles from the Atlanta Braves. The better quality baseball is down the road in Atlanta and not in Gwinnett and this takes fans away from attending Gwinnett Braves games (Feinstein 2014). A typical fan attending a Class A- or Class A Advanced-level baseball game may not be as concerned about the quality of the baseball and will therefore not consider attending a Major League Baseball game and a minor league baseball game at the lowest level of full-season affiliated baseball as the same baseball product.

Finally, we turn our attention to the RIVALS variable, which measures the number of teams within 100 miles of the minor league team in our data set and that are in the same league as that minor league team. The mean value of RIVALS for independent league baseball teams in our data set is 1.5. The null hypothesis that the mean of the variable RIVALS is the same for independent league and Class A-level baseball ($t=-0.36$) cannot be rejected. Alternatively, the null hypothesis that the mean value of RIVALS in the Class A Advanced ($t=-3.02$), Double A ($t=2.08$), or Triple A ($t=4.08$) level baseball is equal to the mean value of RIVALS in independent league baseball is rejected. These results suggest that independent league baseball is structured with a geographic density similar to Class A-level baseball but not similar to the highest three levels of full-season affiliated minor league baseball. Because these are only unconditional results, it is difficult to extend any analysis too far. But there may be a relationship between the possible travel budgets available to these teams, which are likely smaller for Class A and independent league than for the other levels of full-season professional minor league baseball, and the geographic dispersion of the teams in the league.

In each one of the unconditional analyses above, there was at least some evidence that the structure of independent league baseball exhibits features that are similar to the structure of certain levels of affiliated minor league baseball. If independent league baseball, which is not constrained by the Major League Rules imposed by Major League Baseball, is seen as an example of how to optimally lay out the geographic parameters of a minor league, we should be able to gain some insight into how proximity matters in minor league baseball can affect attendance. Providing more control within the analysis can therefore yield results that have a potentially higher level of confidence attached to them. The next step in this analysis, therefore, is to present a conditional model of average attendance at minor league baseball games so that we can isolate more precisely the impact of proximity and geographic dispersion of minor league baseball teams on attendance at minor league baseball games.

Regression Analysis

Now we can begin to build a model to describe average attendance at minor league baseball games. This model will be based on the models found in the literature already that have examined attendance at minor league games (see Gitter and Rhoads 2010, 2011, 2014; Winfree and Fort 2008 and Anthony et al. 2014). We will use some of the variables in our model that we have already used for the unconditional analysis earlier in this chapter. This will allow us to provide a more detailed picture of how minor league baseball is geographically organized in affiliated leagues and independent leagues. Additionally, we include controls for stadium age, league, and a time trend.

The basic model presented here is meant to do two primary things. First, the model is designed to link to previous research on minor league baseball so that a deeper understanding of minor league attendance can be achieved. Providing this link allows us to make some comparisons to the earlier research (Gitter and Rhoads 2010, 2011; Winfree and Fort 2008) while also checking on the adequacy of the model to describe average attendance. Second, the model provides a better path to describe the impact of proximity on minor league attendance. As this is the key feature we are studying throughout this book, the results that come from this model will become a critical part of the story we are telling.

The model here estimates average attendance for minor league baseball teams from 2006 to 2013. Independent league baseball is estimated by itself and each level of affiliated baseball is estimated separately. The model uses random effects and a trend term in addition to the independent variables of interest that will be used to control for things that could impact the demand for attending a minor league baseball game and the quality of the team itself. For example, income, prices, and population are not expected to change much during the time period of the analysis for any individual team, but are likely to vary widely across teams and cities included in the study. As such, controlling for them through a random effects model allows an opportunity to better isolate the impact of the control variables that we are most concerned with.

As discussed earlier in this chapter, MLBdist, MiLBdist, and RIVALS are the three variables that are perhaps most useful in best understanding the effects of proximity among minor league baseball teams. In fact, it is primarily because these variables are essential to our understanding of the model and because they only vary across teams and not within teams that a random effects model is used to estimate the coefficients of all the independent variables. A fixed effects model is generally not the right kind of model to use in a setting like this that requires estimating coefficients for variables that do not vary within the team.

The time trend is meant to pick up any general attendance impacts at the minor league level that have occurred during the time period studied and would be expected to affect all teams in a similar manner. For instance, the general economic downturn—what is sometimes called the Great Recession and hit the labor market and the housing market very hard—occurred towards the start of the data series with the 2008 season data. The impact of the general economic conditions throughout the country on minor league baseball average attendance is not particularly clear because of the underlying reasons fans attend minor league baseball games. Attendance at minor league baseball games reflects a desire to attend a live entertainment event, typically for young families, and the desire to watch a professional baseball game of relatively high quality. The Great Recession could have pushed potential fans away from attending games if family entertainment was the key factor bringing them to minor league games in the first place. A recession would likely lead families to cut their entertainment budget during difficult and uncertain economic times, leading them to make less trips to the minor league stadium for a game. Alternatively, the substitutability between a Major League Baseball game and a minor league baseball game could become more obvious during the Great Recession. People that typically would attend a Major League Baseball game may have substituted a less expensive trip to a minor league baseball game instead to save some money. Introduced into the model as a linear variable, the trend term is simply meant to account for the net movement in average attendance over the time period and effectively serves the same purpose as a year dummy variable.

Winning percentage is included to control for the quality of the minor league team. Seth Gitter and I published a paper in the Journal of Sports Economics in 2010 that found more winning leads to higher average attendance. The effect was rather small, but was consistent with the impact of winning on attendance that Winfree and Fort (2008) found for minor league hockey. Including a control for winning percentage allows a comparison to those earlier studies and can serve as a check on whether or not the model is set up correctly. Also, dummy variables for the league are included. This means that league-specific effects such as regional and even cultural factors will be controlled. For example, it is likely that attendance at the Class A Advanced level in the Florida State League will be driven by different factors—demographics, weather, and tourism, for instance—than for those fans attending Carolina or California League games. Stadium age is included to estimate the effect of new and aging stadiums on attendance at the minor league level. Much work has been done on this phenomenon already for baseball stadiums, including the work I published with Seth Gitter in Contemporary Economic Policy in 2014. There we found a novelty effect for new minor league stadiums that persisted for about a decade. Finally, as in Winfree and Fort (2008) and in the work I have published with Seth Gitter (2010, 2011), it will be noted that a dual-log functional form is used to make calculations and interpretations of the results easier.

Equation (2.1) below shows the variables used in the model. The subscripts used in the model, i and t, indicate team and year, respectively. The dependent variable is lnAVEATT_{it}. StadNew_{it} is a dummy variable, taking a value of one for the year in which the stadium opens and zero otherwise. Stad1_3_{it}, Stad4_5_{it}, and Stad6_10_{it} are also dummy variables and all take a value of one if the stadium is of the same age as the digits in the variable name and zero otherwise. For instance, Stad4_5_{it} takes a value of one if the stadium is 4 years old for team i in year t. This same variable would take a value of zero if instead, for instance, the stadium was 6 years old. The log of winning percentage is lnWinPct_{it} and varies across team and year. lnMLBdist_{it}, lnMiLBdist_{it}, and RIVALS_{it} are the three variables that address proximity concerns as discussed already. The remaining variables are dummy variables taking a value of one if the team is in that league and zero otherwise. The omitted leagues in the four levels of full-season affiliated minor league baseball are the International League in Triple A, the Texas League in Double A, the Florida State League in Class A Advanced, and the South Atlantic League in Class A. In independent league baseball, the omitted league is the Atlantic League. All regression results are included in Table 2.5 below. A brief discussion follows:

$$\begin{aligned}
\text{lnAVEATT}_{it} = {} & \\
& \beta_0 + \beta_1\text{Trend}_t + \beta_2\text{StadNew}_{it} + \beta_3\text{Stad1_3}_{it}\,\beta_4\text{Stad4_5}_{it} + \beta_5\text{Stad6_10}_{it} \\
& + \beta_6\text{lnWinPct}_{it} + \beta_7\text{MLBdist}_{it} + \beta_8\text{MiLBdist}_{it} + \beta_9\text{RIVALS}_{it} \\
& + \beta_{10}\text{Midwest}_{it} + \beta_{11}\text{California}_{it} + \beta_{12}\text{Carolina}_{it} + \beta_{13}\text{Eastern}_{it} + \beta_{14}\text{Southern}_{it} \\
& + \beta_{15}\text{PacificCoast}_{it} + \beta_{16}\text{AmAssoc}_{it} + \beta_{17}\text{CanAm}_{it} + \beta_{18}\text{Frontier}_{it} + \gamma_i + \varepsilon_t
\end{aligned} \tag{2.1}$$

The first observation to note is the general downward trend in average attendance through the time period for the highest levels of minor league baseball. Specifically, the Double A and Triple A levels of affiliated baseball along with independent league baseball show a slight drop in average attendance during the 2006–2013 time period that is attributed to the Trend variable. The drop is not large—ranging between 0.7 and 3.3 % per year—but it is notable that it is different than Class A Advanced-level baseball which experienced a general rise in average attendance of 1.6 % attributed to the Trend variable. There is no significant change in the trend for average attendance at the Class A level. These somewhat mixed results are in line with the prior research on minor league baseball attendance; however the magnitude

Table 2.5 Regression results

	Class A	Class A Advanced	Double A	Triple A	Independent
Trend	−0.004 (0.004)	0.016*** (0.005)	−0.007** (0.003)	−0.013*** (0.003)	−0.033*** (0.006)
StadNew	0.186** (0.083)	0.0744*** (0.133)	0.295*** (0.053)	0.164*** (0.042)	0.156* (0.083)
Stad1_3	0.225*** (0.058)	0.495*** (0.078)	0.199*** (0.036)	0.108*** (0.035)	0.133** (0.066)
Stad4_5	0.141*** (0.051)	0.282*** (0.097)	0.130*** (0.036)	0.067** (0.034)	0.103* (0.057)
Stad6_10	0.037 (0.035)	0.191*** (0.052)	0.051** (0.025)	0.034* (0.019)	0.039 (0.037)
lnWinPct	0.019 (0.054)	−0.114 (0.095)	0.150** (0.060)	0.078 (0.050)	0.185*** (0.065)
lnMLBdist	−0.206 (0.154)	−0.195** (0.097)	−0.172* (0.092)	−0.064 (0.080)	−0.074** (0.036)
lnMiLBdist	0.029 (0.234)	0.055 (0.074)	0.236** (0.097)	−0.133 (0.090)	0.289*** (0.061)
RIVALS	−0.040 (0.045)	−0.082 (0.056)	−0.023 (0.067)	−0.010 (0.125)	0.047* (0.029)
Midwest	−0.082 (0.065)				
California		0.260 (0.263)			
Carolina		0.565* (0.317)			
Eastern			0.117 (0.175)		
Southern			−0.174 (0.136)		
PacificCoast				0.065 (0.125)	
AmAssoc					−0.352*** (0.134)
CanAm					−0.701*** (0.080)
Frontier					−0.587*** (0.107)
Constant	8.974*** (1.118)	8.057*** (0.552)	8.280*** (0.665)	9.644*** (0.523)	7.665*** (0.272)

Standard errors in parentheses
***Significant at the 1 % level
**Significant at the 5 % level
*Significant at the 10 % level

of the trend for independent league baseball is quite a bit larger than it is for any of the levels of affiliated baseball or for the previous research. It is possible that the relatively large trend downward in independent league baseball average attendance is a reflection of the more difficult economic conditions experienced throughout the country impacting professional baseball not affiliated with the most valuable brand in baseball. That is, independent league baseball teams without the Major

League Baseball brand formally attached to them may be more susceptible to changing economic conditions. This would possibly be a function of uncertainty over the quality of the product during economic downturns and opportunity during economic expansions.

The next set of variables to consider are the stadium age indicators. In Table 2.5, this includes all the variables that begin with Stad. These dummy variables take on a value of one during the year for which the age of the stadium is of a particular age. Seth Gitter and I had earlier determined that the novelty effect at minor league baseball stadiums was similar to Major League Baseball stadiums (2014). But the increased attendance from the novelty effect persisted somewhat longer for minor league stadiums, possibly reflecting a relative lack of substitute entertainment opportunities in cities with minor league teams compared to cities with Major League Baseball teams. At all levels of full-season professional minor league baseball from 2006 to 2013, the novelty effect of a new stadium appears to last for at least 5 years. In fact, at the Class A Advanced, Double A, and Triple A levels, this novelty effect is present up to 10 years after a new stadium is built.

These novelty effects are consistent with those that I found with Seth Gitter in our work published in Contemporary Economic Policy in 2014. For example, in that earlier research we had found that Double A attendance increased about 22 % in the first year the minor league team played at the new stadium. For a Triple A team, average attendance increased about 16 % in the first year with the new stadium. Compare these results to those in Table 2.5, where Double A and Triple A average attendance increased 29.5 % and 16.4 %, respectively, in the first year playing in the new stadium. Additionally, the estimated coefficients for the novelty effects for affiliated minor league baseball teams at all levels were remarkably consistent with those coefficients estimated in my work with Seth Gitter.

The one notable difference is that both Class A and independent league baseball teams seem to lose the novelty effect more quickly than the other levels of full-season minor league baseball. While still positive coefficients, they are no longer significant and suggest that there may be more substitutes for the lowest level of full-season affiliated minor league baseball and for independent league baseball. To put it another way, quality matters and the relatively low quality of Class A affiliated baseball and the lack of the Major League Baseball brand to provide a signal of quality are not enough to overcome an aging stadium as novelty effect wears off after just 5 years.

The next variable of interest in our model is lnWinPct. The coefficient on this variable, if significant, lets us know how important winning is to minor league baseball fans. It is not expected to be much different than the prior research on attendance for minor league sports, and this is why building this model like the models in earlier research is helpful. The results in Table 2.5 are fairly close to those that Seth Gitter and I reported in the Journal of Sports Economics (2010). Specifically, the magnitude of the coefficients that are significant is close enough to be in line with that prior research. Note that it is only at the Double A level of affiliated minor league baseball and in independent league baseball where winning seems to directly lead to more fans. In Double A-level and independent league baseball, a 10 % increase in winning percentage leads to an increase in average attendance of 1.5 %

and 1.85 %, respectively. Compare those numbers to 1.9 % and 2.3 % for Class A (both levels) and Double A affiliated baseball found in my work with Seth Gitter (2010). Winfree and Fort (2008) found that increasing winning percentage by 10 % for a minor league hockey team leads to an increase of between 1.5 and 2.2 %. So the results here for Double A and independent league baseball compare well with prior research.

As seen in Table 2.5, the coefficients on lnWinPct for Triple A and both Class A levels of affiliated minor league baseball are not significant. The Triple A result lines up with my work with Seth Gitter (2010) but the results for Class A need some additional explanation. In the previous research, full-season Class A minor league baseball was combined in the model, so the significant results there cannot be perfectly compared to these results in Table 2.5 and we will not place much focus on those results in this current research.

Only a few of the dummy variables on the leagues within each of the levels are significant, suggesting that many of the leagues do not differ much from each other in average attendance. In fact, many of the affiliated minor league baseball teams' marketing departments share ideas for attracting fans to the ballpark. Art Solomon, in his book Making it in the Minors (2012), notes the following: "One of the surprising discoveries that I made in owning a minor league baseball club was to realize that other minor league teams seek to help other affiliated club. Since teams play in different markets miles apart, no overt competition exists for revenue; no rivalry occurs other than on the diamond. To that end, teams willingly share information about promotions that work with their clubs, not only within our specific league, but with all affiliated teams, especially at the Baseball Winter Meetings where the Bob Freitas Seminars remain one of the highlights of the annual event." Solomon's insight into how minor league baseball is marketed to the local fans suggests that many of the same techniques are used within each league. So it is not surprising that with the exception of the Carolina League in Class A Advanced-level baseball, no league effect appears to be present in affiliated minor league baseball.

The last coefficients to examine are those that deal with proximity. In Table 2.5, these are the variables lnMLBdist, lnMiLBdist, and Rivals100. We start by examining the coefficients on the variable measuring the distance to the nearest Major League Baseball team, lnMLBdist. The first thing to note is that the estimated coefficient is negative for each level of affiliated minor league baseball and for independent league baseball. This is not necessarily expected if we are to think of Major League Baseball and minor league baseball as substitutes, as Seth Gitter and I found in our Journal of Sports Economics paper (2010). A negative coefficient on lnMLBdist suggests that closer proximity to a Major League Baseball stadium (smaller value of lnMLBdist) will lead to greater average attendance at minor league baseball games. Without having ticket price data for the independent league teams in the data set, it is simply not possible to include a control which would likely provide an opportunity to determine whether or not these minor league teams are substitutes for Major League Baseball. Instead, it is likely that this coefficient is a reflection of the population of the city in which the minor league team is located. A smaller value of lnMLBdist means closer proximity to a large city and a larger population from which to draw possible minor league baseball fans. But there is also the potential that at the margin, regional brand awareness causes fans to attend more games the closer they live to a Major League Baseball stadium. This would suggest that the recent push by Major League Baseball to regionalize their affiliates could lead to greater attendance for minor league teams. There will be more discussion on this topic in the next few chapters.

The coefficients are significant and reasonably close for both the Class A Advanced and Double A levels. Specifically, a minor league team that is 10 miles closer to a Major League Baseball stadium than another team should expect to attract 1.95 % and 1.72 % more fans per game at the Class A Advanced and Double A levels, respectively. For the average Class A Advanced team, this means that about 46 more fans would attend each game and attendance would increase for the season by about 3,220. The average Double A team would have average attendance increase by about 75 fans and annual attendance would go up by about 5,250. These effects are comparable to that of increasing winning percentage by about 10 %.

Independent league baseball teams experience a smaller effect from being in closer proximity to a Major League Baseball stadium. An independent league team that is 10 miles closer to a Major League Baseball stadium than another independent league team would see about 0.74 % more fans per game. This amounts to about 25 fans per game, or about 1,750 fans per year. The lower increase in attendance is likely a function of not having the Major League Baseball brand attached. To be precise, not having the Major League Baseball brand attached to independent league baseball teams, as it is to affiliated minor league teams, leads to fewer Major League Baseball fans that spill over to attend independent league baseball games that do not have the Major League Baseball brand attached. This result seems to suggest some initial evidence quantifying the proximity value of the Major League Baseball brand at the minor league level.

The second variable in Table 2.5 that helps tell a more complete proximity story is lnMiLBdist. The coefficient on this variable indicates the effect of closer proximity to the nearest affiliated minor league baseball stadium on average attendance. Only at the Triple A level is the estimated coefficient negative; it is positive at all other levels of minor league baseball, including independent league baseball. A positive coefficient on lnMiLBdist means that closer proximity to an affiliated minor league baseball stadium leads to fewer fans. While there is no ticket pricing data in this model, the positive coefficient is consistent with the conclusion that minor league baseball games are substitutes for each other. Note, however, that the lnMiLBdist coefficient is only significant for the Double A level and for independent league teams and has roughly the same value for each of these. A minor league baseball team that is 10 miles closer to an affiliated minor league baseball stadium results in average attendance decreasing by 2.36 % and 2.89 % for Double A and independent league teams, respectively. A decrease in average attendance of approximately 104 fans per game, or about 7,280 fans per year, can be expected for a team at the Double A level. For an independent league team, this closer proximity would be expected to lead to about 86 fewer fans per game, or about 6,000 fans per year.

So far, the results we have examined seem to suggest that independent league baseball teams and Double A-level minor league baseball teams are quite similar in how winning and proximity to Major League Baseball stadiums and affiliated minor league baseball stadiums affect attendance. This is perhaps not that surprising. While every Double A-level baseball team is affiliated with a Major League Baseball team, there is likely a greater disconnect with fans perceiving the players on the team as genuine prospects of the Major League parent team, as compared to both Class A levels and Triple A-level baseball. Many times, the first place a top prospect in the minor league system lands is at a Class A- or Class A Advanced-level team. Alternatively, the last place a top prospect can play minor league baseball is at the Triple A level. That leaves the middle level—Double A-level baseball—to be the player development grounds that fans typically perceive to have the least direct connection between the prospect and the Major League Baseball parent team. Thus, it makes sense that if the coefficients we have examined so far from Table 2.5 are somehow meant to show the value of the Major League Baseball brand, independent league baseball—which has no direct affiliation with Major League Baseball—and Double A-level baseball—which has perhaps the least direct perceived prospect connection with the Major League Baseball parent team—should have similar characteristics.

The last variable we examine in Table 2.5 that is linked to proximity is RIVALS which measures the number of teams in the same league and that are within a 100-mile direct line radius of that minor league team. This variable is meant to generate some insight into how the density (or intensity) of minor league teams affects attendance. Because Major League Rules dictate how close minor league teams are to be to one another, it is expected that more teams within a closer proximity would decrease the number of fans attending games. After all, theory suggests that substitute minor league baseball games should draw fans away. But it is also possible that ticket prices would drop with more teams in closer proximity to each other. Further, fans of rival teams in the same league may want to travel to see a game at the "away" park. These two factors could increase the number of fans at the game and this variable allows us to gain initial insight into this phenomenon.

There are two noteworthy features to report regarding the coefficients of RIVALS. First, all the affiliated levels of minor league baseball have a negative sign on the coefficient while independent league baseball has a positive coefficient. Second, only the coefficient for the independent league baseball model is significant. Increasing by one the number of teams within 100 miles that are in the same league is expected to lead to 4.7 % more fans per game for an independent league team. This means that about 140 additional fans will be expected to attend an independent league baseball game when there is one additional team in the league within 100 miles. Over the course of a season, there would be nearly 10,000 additional fans in attendance for that team. Again, because ticket prices are not included in this model it is not possible to clearly determine how much of the increased attendance is due to fans of other teams in the league attending games at the "away" stadium and how much is due to ticket prices that were bid down as there was more competition to attract baseball fans in an increasingly competitive market. In either case, there is clearly a difference in how proximity to more teams within a league affects attendance for independent league baseball teams compared to affiliated minor league baseball teams.

A few possibilities exist to try to explain why more teams in the same league that are relatively close to an independent league baseball team leads to more fans attending games. The first potential explanation is that with the restrictions placed on affiliated minor league baseball teams to be located in close proximity to each other, maybe independent league baseball is simply filling a market void by fielding multiple teams in locations that can handle more teams than permitted by Major League Baseball rules. This is not to suggest that Major League Baseball and its affiliated minor league teams are not aware of the market setting in which its teams play. But the results do suggest that the elasticity of demand for professional baseball in the communities in which minor league baseball teams are located are uniquely structured to be able to generate robust attendance figures and should not be ignored. That is, more than just the Major League Baseball brand is at work in attracting fans to attend professional baseball games in a minor league setting.

The second potential explanation for why independent league teams are able to generate higher attendance in the presence of more teams in close proximity is the potential for creating and maintaining rivalries between certain teams within the league. Rivalries within sports are often a major incentive to draw fans to attend games and to take an interest in the outcome of game, regardless of the level of success for either team throughout the season. The rivalries between teams such as the New York Yankees and Boston Red Sox and the Los Angeles Dodgers and San Francisco Giants span generations and have a rich history for fans.

While rivalries between teams within independent league baseball would never be expected to compare to rivalries within Major League Baseball, they may lead to higher attendance. The York Revolution and the Lancaster Barnstormers of the Atlantic League play their home games just a 30-min drive from each other and the team with more wins in head-to-head play during the regular season is awarded the Community Cup. This rivalry, formalized in the War of the Roses series, is probably not known beyond the south-central Pennsylvania region. But local rivalries between smaller minor league baseball teams like these may still be able to generate enough fan interest at the margin to cause a noticeable increase in attendance. And while rivalries are always a draw for fans when both teams are doing well in the standings, perhaps rivalries are even more significant for teams during a season when they are not experiencing as much success on the field. That is, rivalries can induce demand which can increase attendance regardless of the success of the teams.

It should be noted that this result is consistent with the most recent move by the Atlantic League to move away from a balanced schedule of games for the 2015 schedule. In announcing the 2015 schedule, Atlantic League president Rick White noted a push towards developing an unbalanced schedule that would both encourage and enhance natural rivalries determined by proximity. Instead of playing each of the other seven teams in the league 20 times, the new Atlantic League schedule allows for teams to play certain teams more than others, highlighting, among other benefits, the natural rivalries that are present due to proximity. In a press release,

White was quoted as observing that "the 2015 schedule underscores [the] effort to emphasize fan engagement by highlighting regional and intra-divisional rivalries." Additionally, the Atlantic League office suggests that scheduling games based largely on proximity will be expected to reduce travel and player development costs.[9] Assuming that the Atlantic League teams have powerful incentives to maximize attendance and revenues, this move towards an unbalanced schedule is entirely consistent with the results I have found in my model and further suggests some policy moves other minor leagues should seriously consider.

The regression analysis in this chapter has allowed us to focus on how proximity matters within minor league baseball effect attendance. Proximity to the closest Major League Baseball team can impact certain levels of affiliated and independent league baseball in similar ways. And proximity to the closest affiliated minor league baseball team highlights similarities between Double A-level baseball and independent league baseball. Finally, attendance at independent league baseball games does not seem to decrease when more teams within the same league are in closer proximity. All of these results together suggest that a nuanced approach to caring about proximity matters for professional baseball teams would seem to be a major influencing factor in what motivates business decisions for minor league baseball executives. The next chapters will switch the focus onto how proximity to affiliated minor league baseball teams can be a major factor influencing business decisions for Major League Baseball executives.

[9] Accessed http://atlanticleague.com/news-league/news-league.aspx?ID=827 on October 30, 2014.

Chapter 3
Regionalization of Affiliated Minor League Teams

In spring 2012, Major League Baseball's Washington Nationals Class A affiliate was the Hagerstown Suns, but the relationship between the two teams was on somewhat shaky ground. A Nationals press release in March 2012 noted that the Nationals had agreed to terms to renew the player development contracts with four of their affiliates: the Syracuse Chiefs (Triple A, International League), the Harrisburg Senators (Double A, Eastern League), the Potomac Nationals (Class A Advanced, Carolina League), and the Auburn Doubledays (Short Season, New York–Penn League). Nationals General Manager Mike Rizzo was quoted in the press release as saying, "… we value our relationships and the environments cultivated by the good people in Syracuse, Harrisburg, Potomac and Auburn. We take our affiliate relations very seriously in Washington. They are a vital part of our family and we know that with time, these bonds will only strengthen."[1]

Noticeably absent from the press release and from Rizzo's comments was any mention of renewing the player development contract with the Suns, which was also set for renewal with the other contracts. The Suns play in Municipal Stadium in Hagerstown, Maryland. The stadium was opened in 1931 and is 64 miles from Nationals Park in Washington. But, according to news reports in fall 2013, the Suns affiliation with the Nationals is expected to change in 2015. The Suns submitted a formal application to minor league baseball and the South Atlantic League in early October 2013 to have their desired move to Fredericksburg, Virginia, approved. News reports say that a $29 million facility—including a 4,750-seat stadium and 20,000 square foot indoor training facility—will be built in time for the start of the 2015 season.[2] Of particular note in this case is that Fredericksburg is just 53 miles away from Nationals Park, while Hagerstown is 64 miles away. So the Nationals

---

[1] Quoted from Nationals press release dated March 16, 2012. The online article was titled, "Nationals Extend Working Agreements with Four Minor-League Affiliates," and was accessed on November 7, 2013.

[2] News from fredericksburg.com article by Bill Freehling titled, "Hagerstown Suns apply to relocate to Fredericksburg," accessed on November 7, 2013.

© Springer Science+Business Media New York 2015
T.A. Rhoads, *The Call Up to the Majors*, Sports Economics, Management and Policy 7, DOI 10.1007/978-1-4614-8924-5_3

will have, in the near future, their Class A affiliate closer to them. There are numerous benefits for a Major League Baseball team being close to its minor league affiliate that we'll highlight later in this chapter. Additionally, the older facilities and field at Municipal Stadium in Hagerstown had been the subject of discussion between the Nationals, the Suns, and Hagerstown town council members for a number of years because of their relatively poor quality. Only a few stadiums in all of affiliated minor league baseball are older than Municipal Stadium, and the Nationals organization was getting concerned about the substandard playing conditions in Hagerstown.[3]

While the move for the Hagerstown Suns to Fredericksburg, Virginia, still has a long way to go, it is informative in helping us to recognize the power that the Washington Nationals hold as a Major League Baseball team with considerable monopoly power. The Suns ownership group indicated that the team is leaving Hagerstown because of pressure the Washington Nationals put on them.[4] And this monopoly power is being used to aid in moving the Nationals Class A affiliate to a state-of-the-art playing facility that is marginally closer. As there are no reports that the Nationals are paying for the move—although they likely engaged in countless hours of planning and negotiation—this story suggests considerable market power for a Major League Baseball team. It also suggests potential benefits that can be generated for the Major League team in the form of improved player development opportunities as the affiliate minor league team is located closer to the front-office staff of the Major League parent team.

Generalizing the Regionalization Story

Doubtless, there are other stories like the one involving the Suns and the Nationals that have not been documented so well in the media. And while we will not elaborate on them here, they would all point to the consistent message offered throughout this book—Major League Baseball's antitrust exemption provides a measure of monopoly power in a number of settings, including the structure and operations of minor league baseball. With no other competing leagues that exist at the highest level of professional baseball due in large part to antitrust exemption, this power can be used by Major League Baseball to restrict quantity produced and increase ticket prices and the value of television broadcast rights. This helps Major League Baseball to maintain its high brand value as the only professional baseball league operating at the highest level. We've already seen that fans attending affiliated minor league

[3] A Ballparkdigest.com article from February 15, 2012 titled, "Suns: Nationals forcing us to move from Hagerstown," and accessed on November 7, 2013, notes, "the Washington Nationals and MLB requested Municipal Stadium meet minimum facility requirements in terms of the playing surface and the clubhouse setups."

[4] A February 15, 2012, article titled, "Suns: Nationals forcing us to move from Hagerstown," and accessed through Ballparkdigest.com begins, "The Hagerstown Suns (Class A; Sally League) say they're leaving Municipal Stadium because of pressure from parent Washington Nationals."

baseball and independent league baseball games behave differently when teams in their same league are located closer to one another. And even though we don't have ticket pricing data to go deeper into what that fan behavior suggests, the results are certainly consistent with Major League Baseball providing affiliated minor league baseball with a higher brand value and an opportunity to keep ticket prices high.

In this chapter, we are going to continue in this arena by examining the economics of the locational choices present in affiliated minor league baseball. By keeping in front of us the monopoly power that Major League Baseball enjoys, we will be able to see some of the ways they are able to make and maintain affiliations with minor league baseball teams in a way that benefits them. We will sharpen our focus on the importance of player development, but not from the standpoint of player salaries and contracts as most previous research has examined. Instead, we will begin to look at the affiliation decisions of Major League Baseball teams at the different levels of minor league baseball and whether or not those decisions seem to be driven by proximity. The focus, therefore, is on determining whether or not Major League Baseball teams seem to be pursuing a consistent and league-wide strategy of minimizing the player development costs that come from travel costs induced by certain affiliation decisions. And recent affiliation changes suggest that Major League Baseball teams may be pursuing a strategy of affiliation with minor league teams that mirrors the strategy the National Football League seems to be using with their franchise locational decisions. We'll discuss more of that phenomenon later.

More and more research is pointing out the benefits that can be realized by a firm with branch or franchise locations that are closer in geographic and travel time proximity to headquarters. Major League Baseball produces professional baseball games at the highest level of play in the world. As such, player development has an important role in the production function for every Major League Baseball team. One strategy of achieving and then maintaining a baseball team of the highest quality is to develop minor league baseball players at the affiliate minor league level before moving them up to the Major League level. This strategy has been in place at least since the 1920s when Branch Rickey began to establish the St. Louis Cardinals farm system (Zimbalist 1992).

Understandably, there are benefits to a Major League Baseball team from affiliating with a minor league team that is in geographically close proximity. All else equal, when an affiliate minor league baseball team is relatively close, player development becomes a goal that can more easily be enforced by the Major League team. Coaching staff and personnel from the Major League team can more easily and more often visit the minor league affiliate to check on the progress of the players in their own farm system. This allows for a stricter adherence to developing players in a manner consistent with the Major League team's philosophy. In short, there is less likelihood for any minor league team's coaches and players to shirk.

That Major League Baseball teams can potentially benefit from affiliations with minor league baseball teams that are in closer proximity should not be surprising. Management oversight of the work crews at branch offices or franchises becomes more difficult and costly as distance from headquarters increases. In fact, the economics literature that points to the benefits of business establishments being in close proximity to the company headquarters is rich and intuitive. We'll take a look now at some of the important results from this literature and make the necessary connections that allow us to begin to focus on the need for Major League Baseball management teams to keep watch on the progress of player development at their affiliate minor league baseball teams.

Local Control?

The ability to manage a work staff is difficult enough when the management team is in the same building as the employees. The fact that dozens of books on business management are published every year, with many on the New York Times bestseller list, suggests that it's not easy to get a group of employees to successfully reach and maintain specific output and performance goals. This task is exacerbated when the staff to be monitored and evaluated is located upwards of hundreds of miles away from headquarters. But this is precisely the situation for many Major League Baseball teams that have affiliate minor league teams located far away and need to be monitored and evaluated. Player development is a critical piece in any team's success, and the distance to the affiliate minor league team is a potential choice variable for many, if not all, Major League Baseball teams.

The economics literature has much to say about this kind of setting in general. For businesses that franchise, franchising can eliminate some of the need for local control, making it more likely that businesses grant franchise agreements in areas that are further from headquarters (Brickley and Dark 1987). More often, company-owned establishments are closer to headquarters; franchised establishments that are under local ownership tend to be further away from headquarters. Additionally, Lafontaine (1992) finds that more franchising occurs for a business with more geographical dispersion. This suggests that business establishments that are spread across a greater area tend to allow for local control—and not headquarters control—in order to proxy for management oversight from company headquarters.

Geographic distance seems to add to the costs of monitoring and organizing the operations at branches or franchises away from headquarters. Ray Kroc, founder of McDonald's, in his 1977 autobiography wrote of the effect on the manager of a local McDonald's store that happened to be within view (with binoculars) of Kroc's home. Kroc notes, with enthusiasm, that the crew of that particular McDonald's worked hard. And that's the point. When the boss has an opportunity to keep close tabs on the work of those responsible for getting the product to market, the work will generally be done well. Closer proximity to a branch or franchise makes this task easier partly because the travel costs involved in monitoring and organizing are lower. More trips from headquarters to the branch office or franchise location can be made, which allows for the necessary monitoring to take place.

A final piece of this literature that we want to highlight is that a branch is more likely to fail the further it is from headquarters, according to research by Kalnins and Lafontaine (2013). They attributed shorter branch establishment longevity to be a function of monitoring costs and local information asymmetries that arise from the owners being further away. Effectively, the further away a branch office is from headquarters, the more costly the monitoring and the poorer the quality of information regarding work performance. Keeping tabs on employees is important, and it becomes more costly the further away management is from the branch office.

The link this literature provides for us to view Major League Baseball's affiliation agreements with minor league baseball teams for player development purposes is helpful. As we look through the lens of local control and player development, there seems to be a better incentive structure to achieve player development goals with local ownership of the minor league team instead of ownership by the Major League Baseball team. And, perhaps for the reasons highlighted by this strand of the economics literature, there has been a movement over the years away from Major League Baseball teams owning their minor league affiliates to local ownership with a formal Player Development Contract that is agreed to by every affiliated minor league baseball team. Zimbalist (1992) notes that while Major League Baseball teams owned 207 of the over 300 minor league baseball teams in existence in 1951, only 38 minor league teams were owned in 1957 by a Major League Baseball team. And these numbers have not deviated significantly since then. The St. Louis Cardinals and Atlanta Braves are some of the few Major League Baseball teams that are owners of some of their minor league affiliate baseball teams. But they are clearly not the norm, and most every minor league baseball team at the low A level and above are owned and operated by a person or group other than a Major League Baseball team. Table 3.1 provides the list of the nine minor league teams from the Class A level and above that are owned by their Major League parent club. With 120 minor league teams at these levels of professional baseball, it is clear that local control over the daily operations of the minor league baseball team is most prevalent.

That almost all affiliated minor league baseball teams are independently owned should not be surprising given what the economics literature tells us about the benefits that can come from local control of a business. Note that two proximity characteristics can generally be found across the affiliations listed in the table above. With the exception of the Mississippi Braves, either the minor league affiliate is located relatively close to the Major League parent team—within 150 miles of the

Table 3.1 Major league team ownership of minor league affiliate team in 2014

Level	League	Minor league team	Major league team owner
Triple A	International	Gwinnett Braves	Atlanta Braves
Double A	Southern	Mississippi Braves	Atlanta Braves
Double A	Texas	Springfield Cardinals	St. Louis Cardinals
Class A Advanced	Florida State League	Clearwater Threshers	Philadelphia Phillies
Class A Advanced	Florida State League	Jupiter Hammerheads	Miami Marlins
Class A Advanced	Florida State League	Lakeland Flying Tigers	Detroit Tigers
Class A Advanced	Florida State League	Palm Beach Cardinals	St. Louis Cardinals
Class A Advanced	Florida State League	Tampa Yankees	New York Yankees
Class A	South Atlantic	Rome Braves	Atlanta Braves

parent team—or the minor league affiliate plays in the spring training facility of their Major League parent team.[5] In those cases of close locational proximity, we must assume that proximity is beneficial to evaluating and enforcing the progress of player development. Major League team ownership, and not local ownership, is consistent with a "branch" location that is closer in proximity. The other affiliations noted in the table above suggest that checking on the progress of player development is not quite as important if the training facilities are the best in the industry. Given that the Major League-level players in the organization use the minor league affiliates' facilities to prepare for the season while at the spring training facility, Major League team executives responsible for player development are likely to place a high value on training facilities over locational proximity. In both cases noted, player development is likely an important piece of the decision making that takes place.

In the FAQs section of the business of minor league baseball website, a description of what goes into creating affiliations between Major League Baseball teams and minor league affiliates provides useful insight into this issue. Below is the text from that website.

Q. If a minor league team signs a Player Development Contract with a different MLB organization, rather than renewing an existing agreement, will the team have to relocate?

A. The Player Development Contract creates an affiliation between a Major League organization and the ownership of a minor league franchise. Though many stadiums are built, owned, and managed by local municipalities—often to attract or retain a minor league team—most MiLB franchise owners are private individuals or ownership groups. Some Major League organizations may own one or more of their minor league teams, but this is not necessarily widespread. The decision to begin the relocation process is made by the franchise owner of the minor league baseball club. It is often—but not necessarily—connected to signing a new PDC. Some factors affecting a team's decision to relocate might be attendance, stadium conditions and leases, geographical proximity to other clubs in the same league or to its Major League parent, climate conditions, economic landscape of its local market, etc.[6]

One key point to note in the above answer to the FAQ is that location decisions are made with an eye towards proximity of the minor league team to its Major League parent club. And, of course, there are many factors impacting that locational choice. These factors include enhancing and increasing the media presence of the Major League Baseball team in local and regional markets around the minor league baseball team along with providing a reasonable opportunity for coaching staff from the parent Major League Baseball team to check on player development at the minor league level. Our empirical focus here will be on the player development consideration to the locational decision, but we must also acknowledge that more precise

[5] Given that the Atlanta Braves own and operate two of their other minor league affiliates at the low A level and higher, it is likely that they own and operate the Mississippi Braves, which are approximately 350 miles away from Atlanta, partly based on organizational preference.

[6] Accessed from http://www.milb.com/milb/info/faq.jsp?mc=business on March 3, 2014.

analytical tools besides descriptive statistics will be necessary to tease out the likely impact of player development opportunities on locational proximity with the minor league affiliate. We'll be looking more closely at the current state of locational proximity for Major League Baseball teams and their minor league affiliates.

As we have previously noted, Major League Baseball teams enter into an agreement with each of their minor league affiliates using a rather standard Player Development Contract. This Player Development Contract can provide a Major League team with a mechanism to require their currently affiliated minor league team to make some changes in the quality of the facilities that are available for the crop of players in the minor league system. It also provides "cover" for the Major League team to seek an affiliation with another minor league team that may be closer to the Major League team.

Consistently pursuing the ideals espoused by a player development philosophy requires buy-in from every layer of the Major League organization. From the day a player is drafted by an organization, there has to be a commitment by coaches and staff to a development philosophy for it to have and maintain value. This commitment will be seen in more than just what is taught to the players about playing the game of baseball. There are, for example, different philosophies among organizations concerning the importance of sacrifice bunting and base running. But just as important is how the players and coaches are taught and how strictly those teachings are enforced. To be sure, the closer the Major League team is to each of its minor league affiliates, the easier it will be to enforce any kind of player development philosophy that exists within the organization. In the next section, we take a look at two Major League organizations—the Baltimore Orioles and the St. Louis Cardinals—whose player development philosophies are noteworthy for the consistency of application and the quality of Major League player that is produced. But more pertinent to what we want to examine here, we focus on how these two organizations are among the Major League leaders in geographic proximity to their minor league affiliates. Deciding how important that proximity is to player development will be left to future research. Here, we simply identify some general trends and make some more casual observations.

The Cardinal Way and the Oriole Way

There are a few examples of Major League Baseball organizations that, from top to bottom, try to push a consistent philosophy of player development and are noted for it. In this section, we highlight the Baltimore Orioles and St. Louis Cardinals organizations. In particular, we focus our attention on just one element of the organizational structure of their minor league systems—the distance from the Major League team to each of the minor league affiliates from the Class A level on up. Later in this chapter, we expand our look at affiliate proximity to the rest of Major League Baseball and provide a more general analysis of this important element in player development.

The Orioles and Cardinals organizations have been fairly successful at producing Hall of Fame caliber players and World Series championships for a number of years. For example, the Baltimore Orioles have espoused developing players at all levels of their minor league organization the "Oriole Way," which places a focus on developing fundamentally sound professional baseball players. At least part of this organizational philosophy can be attributed to Cal Ripken, Sr., the father of Hall of Famer, and Iron Man, Cal Ripken, Jr. Hall of Famers Brooks Robinson, Eddie Murray, and Cal Ripken, Jr., were all a product of the "Oriole Way." The Orioles in 2013 had one of the youngest rosters in the Major Leagues. Their pitching staff had an average age of 27.9 years old, which was 0.5 years younger than the league average. Ten Major League teams had pitching staffs that were younger. Orioles batters averaged 27.7 years old, which was tied for the fourth youngest in the Majors. Manny Machado, who at the age of 21 earned an All-Star appearance and a Gold Glove award in his first full year in Major League Baseball, now exemplifies the best of the current "Oriole Way" in player development (Crasnick 2013).

Some have suggested that the "Cardinal Way" is one of the main reasons the St. Louis Cardinals continue to be postseason contenders despite being in a mid-major market without the luxury of seemingly limitless dollars for player payroll. At about $115 million in 2013, the Cardinals payroll was exceeded by ten Major League Baseball teams and was about $12 million more than the league average. The Boston Red Sox, who beat the Cardinals four games to two in the 2013 World Series, paid their players an average of $1 million more than the Cardinals and the median Cardinal salary of about $1.5 million was over $2 million less than the Red Sox median salary.

Yet despite the Cardinals not having one of the highest payrolls in Major League Baseball, they have found success through player development. Tony Calandro (2013) notes that each player drafted by the St. Louis Cardinals organization receives an 86-page handbook on player conduct on and off the field. No Major League Baseball team since 2000 has won more postseason baseball games than the St. Louis Cardinals. And while I am not proposing here that a statistically significant causal relationship exists between the "Cardinal Way" and the success of the Cardinals organization, there is likely some level of success for the St. Louis Cardinals that comes from their rigorous organizational structure. That the "Cardinal Way" has been written down and distributed to players and coaches in the Cardinals organization suggests that player development models matter. And if player development matters, then it follows that enforcing the player development model for an organization matters as well. By motivating the topic of player development in this manner, we can begin to highlight the benefits that geographic proximity can make in getting professional baseball players ready for the Major Leagues.

Let's take a closer look at the Orioles and Cardinals minor league organizations and focus now on the geographic proximity of the Major League team to each of its minor league affiliates from the Class A level up. The table below lists these distances, in miles, for the Orioles and Cardinals. We'll examine all of the Major League teams later in this chapter.

Starting with the Orioles, their minor league affiliates in 2013 from Triple A down to Class A ball were the Norfolk Tides, the Bowie Baysox, the Frederick

Keys, and the Delmarva Shorebirds. The distances from Oriole Park at Camden Yards, where the Orioles play home games in Baltimore, to each of their affiliated minor league teams were the lowest total distance in all of Major League Baseball. The Orioles are fortunate to be located in close proximity to minor league teams at the levels of affiliated baseball from Class A up, and to have affiliations with them. Not only do the Orioles enjoy affiliations with minor league teams that are in closer proximity than the average Major League Baseball team by a long shot, but they also have affiliations with the closest minor league teams at each of the Triple A, Double A, and Class A Advanced levels. And their Class A affiliate, the Delmarva Shorebirds, is their second closest minor league team at that level. In other words, the Orioles are affiliates with just about all of minor league teams that are closest to them.

For sure, the Orioles are unusual in having a minor league system with each of their affiliates as close as they are. The average distance in miles to Triple A, Double A, Class A Advanced, and Class A affiliates are 350, 601, 680, and 719 miles, respectively. So a Major League Baseball team whose Triple A minor league affiliate is the average distance away would have a greater travel distance to that one affiliate than the combined distance of all four of the highest level affiliates for the Baltimore Orioles (300 miles). In terms of providing a setting where there is a consistent philosophy of player development up and down the entire organization, the Baltimore Orioles could not imagine a better scenario based on proximity alone.

The St. Louis Cardinals are situated similarly to the Baltimore Orioles with respect to the proximity of their minor league affiliates with the exception of their Class A Advanced affiliate. The Cardinals Triple A, Double A, Class A Advanced, and Class A affiliates are the Memphis Redbirds, the Springfield Cardinals, the Palm Beach Cardinals, and the Peoria Chiefs. As shown in Table 3.2, while the distance from the Cardinals to their affiliates is greater at each level than the Orioles, those distances are generally less than the average distance to affiliate in all but the Class A Advanced level. And, importantly, the Triple A, Double A, and Class A affiliates are either the closest in their level or the second closest. In the case of the Triple A level, the Indianapolis Indians are the Cardinals closest minor league team at that level, but they are only about 12 miles closer than the Cardinals are to their affiliate, the Memphis Redbirds.

Finally, the Class A Advanced minor league team closest to the St. Louis Cardinals is the Salem Red Sox of the Carolina League. They are located 556 miles away in Salem, Virginia, and have been affiliated with the Boston Red Sox since 2009. Given that the closest minor league team is more than 550 miles away from St.

Table 3.2 Distance, in miles, from MLB team to minor league affiliate and proximity rank in parentheses

Level	Baltimore Orioles	St. Louis Cardinals	MLB average
Triple A	169 (1)	240 (2)	350
Double A	25 (1)	196 (1)	601
Class A Advanced	18 (1)	995 (20)	680
Class A	88 (2)	144 (1)	719

Louis, Cardinals staff associated with player development would likely travel to any minor league affiliate by plane, and not by car. For teams like St. Louis that are located in the midwest, there are not any minor league teams close to them—that is, relatively easy driving distance away—at the Class A Advanced level since the three leagues at that level are the California, Carolina, and Florida State Leagues. None of the teams competing in those leagues are within easy driving distance of St. Louis. But despite the lack of minor league teams at the Class A Advanced level that are close to St. Louis, there is a second best option that the Cardinals organization seems to have taken advantage of. While their Class A Advanced affiliate, the Palm Beach Cardinals, are one of the farthest minor league teams at that level from St. Louis, they do happen to play in the same facility in Jupiter, Florida, where the Cardinals have their spring training facilities. This suggests a second best option that is available to the Cardinals and some other teams with affiliates in the Class A Advanced Florida State League where the Grapefruit League of spring training takes place. In taking this approach, the St. Louis Cardinals organization can provide their young players in their minor league system with a Major League quality training facility to help improve their skills.

The Baltimore Orioles and St. Louis Cardinals organizations are somewhat well known for their focus on a consistent player development philosophy through all levels of their minor league affiliates. The "Oriole Way" and the "Cardinal Way" are taught to players in their respective organizations from the day they are drafted. And the relative close proximity to their minor league affiliates is not expected to harm any efforts to enforce the application of these player development philosophies at all levels of play in their minor league system. Coaches and other staff from the Orioles and Cardinals organizations should have every opportunity to travel at relatively low cost to each of their minor league affiliates to check on the progress of player development. This likely minimizes shirking and keeps the player development philosophy consistent. But the Orioles and the Cardinals are perhaps the two Major League Baseball organizations with the best set of minor league affiliates to achieve this kind of approach to player development. Let's now look at proximity to minor league affiliates for Major League Baseball teams more generally.

Proximity and Limiting Major League Baseball Substitutes

Just how close are affiliated minor league baseball teams from their Major League parent team? Because Major League Baseball has a relatively large measure of monopoly power, they have been able to successfully craft regulations regarding where an affiliated professional baseball team may be located. The regulations specify guidelines for proximity to any affiliated baseball team, whether it be a Major League team or a minor league team. And the commissioner of Major League Baseball must ultimately give his approval to these locational decisions.

Having the ability to maintain control over where other professional baseball teams can locate suggests that Major League Baseball teams will maintain considerable power in generating profits above and beyond those expected in a more competitive setting. This is the power that allows Major League Baseball teams to sell tickets at a higher price than if there were competitors in the same geographic market. And because ticket prices are likely higher with this monopoly power, fewer tickets will be sold. Smaller stadiums can be built that create a more intimate feel for fans at the ballpark. Fewer available seats also leaves less opportunity to attend a Major League Baseball game in person, which can increase television viewers and thus increase television ratings and television revenue.

Of course, this line of logic is only necessary if Major League Baseball teams collectively view other professional baseball teams in close geographic proximity as possible substitute goods. That is, baseball fans that attend games at the stadium or watch on television are faced with a choice of which game to attend or watch when there are numerous teams to choose from. And this choice can be based on a number of different criteria—ticket price, concession quality and price, parking, location, quality of team, and competition—that will impact where a fan spends his or her money.

At least two papers in the last 10 years clearly point out that proximity to a Major League Baseball team matters and that professional baseball substitutes for Major League Baseball can adversely impact attendance. The first paper, by Winfree et al. in the October 2004 issue of *Applied Economics*, notes the strong relationship between attendance and location in Major League Baseball. Specifically, their research shows that as the distance between Major League Baseball teams increases, attendance increases as well. This is an observation that is consistent with the story that fans treat Major League Baseball games as substitute goods. All else equal, fans will make a decision based on proximity to the game.

The second paper is one that my coauthor, Seth Gitter, and I published in the December 2010 issue of *Journal of Sports Economics*. In that paper, we found evidence that was consistent with the notion that fans treat Major League Baseball and minor league baseball as substitutes. The results showed that the closest Major League Baseball team is a substitute for minor league baseball teams within 100 miles of that Major League team. Together, these two papers suggest that professional teams in affiliated baseball pose a threat to Major League Baseball ticket sales if the teams are too close to each other. By having antitrust exemption, Major League Baseball is able to control the geographic spacing of professional affiliated baseball teams in order to maximize ticket sales and thus increase the revenue stream of Major League Baseball teams. In other words, Major League Baseball is able to negate, if possible, the negative impact from possible substitutes on attendance by restricting those possible substitutes in the first place.

Major League Baseball Proximity Rules

The rules are clearly laid out in Major League Rules for how home territories are determined for both Major League and minor league baseball teams. With some exceptions, each Major League Baseball team and minor league baseball team is granted "protected territorial rights" by Major League Baseball that provides a unique home territory. Under Rule 52(a)(4) in the Major League Rules and with exceptions and certain allowances, these home territories provide that "No Major or Minor League Club may play its home games within the home territory or within 15 miles from the boundary of the home territory of any other Minor League Club, and no Minor League Club may play its home games within the home territory or within 15 miles of the home territory of any Major League Club."

There is at least one obvious reason for Rule 52(a)(4) to be in place. Owners of Major League Baseball teams and owners of their affiliated minor league teams have every incentive to earn as much profit as possible from running their baseball teams. And given Major League Baseball's antitrust exemption, these owners seem to be exhibiting rational behavior by placing locational limitations on teams in affiliated baseball. Locational limitations are an easy mechanism to maximize those profits—they are easy to enforce and in most cases they are easy to justify. And locational limitations provide for an easy way to effectively limit the choices facing fans when deciding on attending a baseball game in person. The costs of attending a game are real and increase, all else equal, with distance to the stadium. By limiting the set of affiliated baseball games to attend, Major League Baseball becomes very effective in forcing fans to attend specific baseball games. With either limited or no competition in the live professional baseball game market, Major League Baseball can charge higher prices for tickets, and thus earn higher profits.

The Trade-Off in Proximity and Player Development

While it is fairly obvious that Major League Baseball teams want to limit locational choices for other affiliated professional baseball teams by forcing potential competitors away from the local market, there turns out to be a trade-off when it comes to limiting the proximity of Major League and their affiliated minor league baseball teams that serve as player development grounds. Namely, while it is advantageous to locate affiliated minor league baseball teams close to the parent Major League team to keep player development travel costs low, there is a possibility that the affiliated minor league team could take away some of the fans that would otherwise attend the Major League game. Gifis and Sommers, in their paper in *Atlantic Economic Journal* in 2006, suggested that minor league baseball fans had an inherent interest in baseball's roots; they were primarily fans of the game of baseball. So it is entirely possible, and probably likely, that minor league baseball teams can take away fans from Major League teams if they were to move closer to the Major League stadium. Thus, Major League Rule 52(4)(a) is not without some rational concern for lost revenue.

In fact, let me refer once again to the research that Seth Gitter and I published in the *Journal of Sports Economics* in December 2010. In that paper, we found evidence that is consistent with the notion that minor league baseball serves as a substitute for Major League Baseball games. This research points to a very real trade-off that exists when Major League Baseball expresses a desire to locate affiliate minor league teams relatively close to their parent club's stadium. Namely, local fans may opt to attend the minor league baseball game at the stadium closer to them instead of the Major League game at a more distant stadium. And this could cause revenue to drop for the Major League team.

From a research standpoint, there is still room to examine this trade-off more closely. To my knowledge, no one has attempted to determine with any degree of precision just how much revenue is lost for a Major League team as minor league teams locate closer to them. Winfree et al. in their 2004 *Applied Economics* paper made these calculations for Major League teams moving closer to other Major League teams. But because there haven't been any attempts that I am aware of to estimate the travel costs for staff to check on player development at minor league affiliates, it may be worthwhile to develop an initial look at the proximity of minor league baseball teams in comparison to their Major League parent team. But from observing recent moves of some Major League teams, these revenue losses and travel costs related to player development are likely not insignificant. In any case, there still seems to be a need to better understand this trade-off with more research.

A New Direction

While there is still room for developing an expanded research agenda to tease out the precise amounts that can be counted as costs and benefits for a Major League baseball team located closer to their minor league affiliates, I am taking a more basic and general approach here. That is, I am going to attempt to develop a baseline understanding of where Major League Baseball stands today regarding the locational decisions of their minor league affiliates. There has been movement in the past 10 to 15 years, or so, of minor league affiliates that suggests that Major League teams are trying to cut the distance between their stadium and at least some of their affiliates. A relevant question to ask, therefore, is whether Major League Baseball teams' locational choices have changed over that time? Determining where things stand today, and whether or not Major League Baseball teams, in general, have moved their affiliations closer to them will help tell a more nuanced story of just how expansive the reach of Major League Baseball's antitrust exemption extends.

Let us now begin our look at the locational aspects—that is, proximity—of Major League Baseball teams and their minor league affiliates. Each of the 30 Major League Baseball teams has had one affiliate minor league team at each of the minor league levels from Class A and up since 2003. Prior to that, there were some years where some teams had more than one affiliate at a particular level, leaving them with no affiliate at another minor league level. For example, in 2002 the Houston Astros had two affiliate teams—the Lexington Legends and the Michigan Battle Cats (who were then renamed the Battle Creek Yankees, then the Southwest Michigan Devil Rays, and then moved to Midland, MI, are now the Great Lake Loons and affiliated with the Los Angeles Dodgers)—in Class A level and none in Class A Advanced level. In an attempt to keep consistent in our look at minor league affiliates, we are restricting our statistics to 2003 and forward.

Class A Affiliations and Proximity

To start, we'll take a look at the Class A-level affiliations since 2003. Perhaps the most obvious reflection of the lack of a national stage for minor league baseball is that there are only two leagues at the Class A level—the Midwest League and the South Atlantic League. Their names suggest that many of the baseball fans around the country are without an opportunity to be in close proximity to minor league baseball played at the Class A level. There are demographic and market reasons for this that cannot be ignored. With higher levels of professional baseball available in the country, Class A-level baseball is better served in smaller cities, which can have the unwelcome effect of limiting the number of fans that can attend these games.

These demographic concerns are not lost on Major League Baseball, as the Major League Rules provide guidance for stadium size at the different levels of minor league baseball that vary with level. In fact, Attachment 58 to the Major League Rules notes that seating capacities for minor league stadiums should be "appropriate for the size of the Minor League Team's market." The suggested stadium size for minor league stadiums is included in Table 3.3. Note that at 4,000 seats, the Class A stadium recommended seating capacity is just 40 % of the Triple A level, which is a reflection of the smaller size of the typical Class A city compared to the Triple A city. So Class A-level minor league baseball is played in smaller cities around the country, which limits the possible locations for these teams given the locational restrictions Major League Baseball additionally imposes on these teams.

Because city size and location constraints limit locational possibilities, and because regional minor leagues have unique geographic demands for travel and rivalry purposes, some areas of the country that are able to play host to a Major League Baseball team may not be able to do the same for a minor league team. As a result, there is a strong likelihood that minor leagues serving a specific level of professional baseball will be insufficient to match up with the existing Major League cities. This suggests that despite the best intentions of planners, there will be some holes when it comes to aligning minor league teams with Major League teams for affiliation purposes, and we probably see that most clearly at the Class A level.

Because there are just two leagues at the Class A level, and because the geographic scope of these leagues is limited because of travel and rivalry demands, not many Major League teams line up close in proximity to the teams in the Midwest and South Atlantic Leagues. Of the four most significant minor league levels, the Class A-level affiliates as a whole are the furthest from their Major League parent club. At an average of 719 miles from the parent club, Class A-level teams are characterized by not being within close traveling distance to their affiliate Major League

Table 3.3 Minor league recommended stadium seating capacity

Minor league level	Recommended stadium seating capacity
Triple A	10,000
Double A	6,000
Class A	4,000

team. This is perhaps not surprising, as the demographics characterizing Class A-level teams and Major League teams are perhaps as different as can be.

But in spite of the dissimilar traits of Major League and Class A-level cities, there does seem to be a push in recent years towards aligning Major League teams to affiliates that are either the closest available or at least within relatively close traveling distance. In 2003 there were six Major League Baseball teams that had affiliations with the Class A team that was closest to them. In 2013, this number increased to eight, but that increase came after nearly a decade of being at just four or five teams. So it remains to be seen if this increase in aligning Major League teams with the closest Class A-level team is a permanent shift in policy.

It is the case that some teams are the closest Class A-level team to more than one Major League Baseball team. But because each of these minor league teams can be an affiliate for just one Major League team, there will be some instances where a Major League team is not an affiliate with the minor league baseball team closest to them at that level. For example, the Hagerstown Suns in the South Atlantic League are the closest Class A-level team to both the Baltimore Orioles and the Washington Nationals. Because the Suns can only be an affiliate to one Major League team, either one or both of the Orioles and the Nationals must align their affiliation with a Class A-level team that is not closest to them. In this particular case, the Washington Nationals are affiliates with the Suns and the Orioles are affiliates with the Delmarva Shorebirds.

There are at least a few interesting points to note here. The Shorebirds—located in Salisbury, Maryland—are the Class A-level team that is second closest to the Orioles. Oriole Park at Camden Yards is 62 miles from Hagerstown, Maryland, where the Suns play; it is 88 miles from Salisbury, Maryland, where the Shorebirds play. This difference of just 26 miles is perhaps an extra hour in the car with heavy traffic, but being affiliated with the Shorebirds allows the Orioles to get their brand onto Maryland's Eastern Shore. And given the request in October 2013 by the Suns to move their team to Fredericksburg, Virginia, even if the Orioles had been affiliated with the Suns because it was the closest minor league team, the new distance to Fredericksburg wouldn't be any different than it is currently to Salisbury.

Although the above points are specific to the situation with the Orioles and their Class A-level affiliate, there is a more general observation that can be applied to all Major League Baseball teams. There are more benefits that accrue to a Major League team when it comes to its lining up affiliations with minor league teams that stretch beyond simply close proximity that permits lower travel costs in player development. Sometimes the minor league affiliate can help advertise the Major League team to a specific demographic group or geographic market that may otherwise be difficult to reach. There are clearly limits to these benefits, but in some instances, the additional brand exposure can lead to more fans of the Major League team, and can therefore lead to more revenue for that team.

No doubt, there are benefits from aligning with the closest minor league team at a specific level. But often, there are at least a few other teams at the same minor league level that are close enough to provide low travel cost opportunities for player development purposes even if those teams are not the closest. Additionally, because those minor league teams can extend the Major League team's brand further away from the home territory for the parent club, the Major League team can potentially generate higher stadium and television revenues from this brand awareness expansion.

If we expand our look at the proximity characteristics of minor league affiliates at the Class A level to their parent Major League club, we can get a fuller picture of how Major League Baseball may be engaged in an attempt to align affiliates more closely on the map. Assuming that driving a car to a minor league affiliate that is less than 175 miles away is not an overly taxing endeavor for a member of a Major League coaching staff, we can define a minor league affiliate as being close if it is within 175 miles of its Major League parent club. That is, provided that the minor league affiliate is within about a 3- or 4-h drive away, we can assume that it is close enough for a coach or someone from the front office on the Major League team to drop by at virtually any time to spot-check on player development.

Admittedly, the 175-mile proximity definition may be considered by some as arbitrary. But this cutoff is used in an attempt to get at coaches and front-office management personnel having the option to drop in virtually any time unannounced to the minor league affiliate. Having the ability to spot-check on the minor league affiliate in this fashion can solidify the commitment to a consistent player development strategy at all levels of the organization. Essentially, the minor league coaching staff will be less likely to shirk when they know they could be observed at any time by their bosses.

By expanding our definition in this fashion of what it means for a Major League team to be close to its minor league affiliate, we can get a broader picture of the movement that has been made in the past decade of aligning the Class A-level minor league teams with Major League affiliates. As noted above, six Major League teams were affiliates in 2003 with the Class A-level team that was closest to them. Additionally, three more Major League teams were affiliates with Class A-level teams that were located within 175 miles of the parent club. One decade later, in 2013, there were eight Major League teams with the closest Class A-level team as their affiliate and four more Major League teams that had an affiliate within 175 miles of them. So, in the 10 years from 2003 to 2013, Major League Baseball increased by one-third, from 9 to 12, the number of teams affiliated with either the closest Class A-level team or one within 175 miles of them.

Assessing whether or not this apparent move to align Class A-level teams with close Major League Baseball teams has been successful is not an easy task. First, there is the matter of how success is defined. An easy metric is to track the number of Major League Baseball teams that are affiliates with either the closest minor league team at a certain level or at least close to one, with close being defined as within 175 miles. Increasing this number would, of course, indicate that Major League Baseball teams would be moving in the direction of regionalization of minor league affiliates.

But being affiliated with the closest minor league baseball team is not necessarily indicative of being close. Nor is being affiliated with a team that is far down the proximity list an indicator of poor alignment and planning. For instance, the Detroit Tigers are affiliates with the West Michigan Whitecaps, which play their home games at Fifth

Third Ballpark in Comstock Park, Michigan. These two teams are 142 miles apart, and there are four Class A-level teams that are closer to Tigers Stadium than the Whitecaps home stadium. So while the Tigers are not affiliates with the closest minor league team at the Class A level (or even the second, third, or fourth closest team), they are still relatively close in geographic proximity to their affiliate. Contrast the Tigers situation to that to the Minnesota Twins, whose affiliate at the Class A level is the Cedar Rapids Kernels. The Kernels are the closest Class A-level team to the Twins, and yet the stadiums of these two teams are 225 miles apart.

The lesson to learn by looking at the Tigers and the Twins affiliates is that aligning a set of 30 Major League teams with minor league teams can be very complicated as there are many permutations and constraints that must be sorted out. For one Major League team to switch away from an affiliation with a minor league team, there must be at least one other team that switches as well. While it should be the case that all the Major League teams involved in the switch will be made better off after the affiliation change, it is not always the case that the switch will result in a zero-sum game regarding geographic proximity. Because of the nature of the alignment of affiliations and all the parameters that are involved in determining what the right affiliate is, there can be a host of optimization schemes that become available. Trying to solve for a Nash equilibrium alignment of affiliations for 30 Major League teams and 30 minor league teams would be quite an arduous task if we were to take all the parameters of affiliation into account. But if regionalization of affiliates is of primary concern and we restrict ourselves to making close geographic proximity the critical parameter in establishing affiliations, there are some Pareto improvements that could be made. We'll look at a few possible Pareto efficient affiliation switches that could be made later in this book.

Despite the discussion above regarding a push towards regionalization and what looks like some positive gains in that arena, there are some Major League teams for which the only reasonable means of travel to an affiliate minor league team is by air. This leads us to the second point to make regarding how to measure success in regionalizing minor league affiliates—there is likely no real advantage in trying to align west coast teams with their closest Class A-level team as the distance will still be far in excess of 175 regardless of what team is considered. After all, minor leagues with names like South Atlantic and Midwest are not exactly going to have a large number of teams close to west coast Major League Baseball teams.[7] Notice in Table 3.4 how both the Los Angeles Angels of Anaheim and the Baltimore Orioles in 2013 were affiliates with the Class A-level team that was second closest to them. Only 88 miles separate Oriole Park at Camden Yards from Arthur W. Perdue Stadium in Salisbury, Maryland, where the Delmarva Shorebirds play their home games. Under most settings, that is not an overly restrictive constraint on staff to travel from Baltimore to Salisbury, so the expectation is that player development the

[7] For years, names of leagues or divisions did not always line up well with geographic reality. For example, from 1969 to 1993, the Atlanta Braves and Cincinnati Reds were in the National League West Division, while the Chicago Cubs and St. Louis Cardinals were in the National League East Division.

Table 3.4 Proximity rank of 2013 minor league affiliates

Major league team	Triple A affiliate (proximity rank)	Double A affiliate (proximity rank)	Class A Advanced affiliate (proximity rank)	Class A affiliate (proximity rank)
Arizona	Reno (6)	Mobile (11)	Visalia (7)	South Bend (9)
Atlanta	Gwinnett (1)	Mississippi (9)	Lynchburg (5)	Rome (1)
Baltimore	Norfolk (3)	Bowie (1)	Frederick (1)	Delmarva (2)
Boston	Pawtucket (1)	Portland (3)	Salem (5)	Greenville (17)
Chicago Cubs	Iowa (5)	Tennessee (5)	Daytona (9)	Kane County (1)
Chicago White Sox	Charlotte (13)	Birmingham (11)	Winston-Salem (3)	Kannapolis (25)
Cincinnati	Louisville (1)	Pensacola (19)	Bakersfield (27)	Dayton (1)
Cleveland	Columbus (2)	Akron (1)	Carolina (7)	Lake County (1)
Colorado	Colorado Springs (1)	Tulsa (1)	Modesto (8)	Asheville (18)
Detroit	Toledo (1)	Erie (2)	Lakeland (11)	West Michigan (5)
Houston	Oklahoma City (3)	Corpus Christi (1)	Lancaster (25)	Quad Cities (9)
Kansas City	Omaha (1)	Northwest Arkansas (2)	Wilmington (6)	Lexington (13)
Los Angeles Angels	Salt Lake (5)	Arkansas (8)	Inland Empire (3)	Burlington (2)
Los Angeles Dodgers	Albuquerque (6)	Chattanooga (14)	Rancho Cucamonga (1)	Great Lakes (14)
Miami	New Orleans (3)	Jacksonville (1)	Jupiter (1)	Greensboro (9)
Milwaukee	Nashville (8)	Huntsville (9)	Brevard County (14)	Wisconsin (3)
Minnesota	Rochester (11)	New Britain (21)	Fort Myers (18)	Cedar Rapids (1)
New York Mets	Las Vegas (26)	Binghamton (4)	St. Lucie (15)	Savannah (20)
New York Yankees	Scranton (2)	Trenton (1)	Tampa (14)	Charleston (18)
Oakland	Sacramento (1)	Midland (1)	Stockton (2)	Beloit (6)
Philadelphia	Lehigh Valley (1)	Reading (2)	Clearwater (13)	Lakewood (1)
Pittsburgh	Indianapolis (10)	Altoona (1)	Bradenton (15)	West Virginia (3)
San Diego	Tucson (3)	San Antonio (2)	Lake Elsinore (1)	Fort Wayne (11)
San Francisco	Fresno (2)	Richmond (22)	San Jose (1)	Augusta (19)
Seattle	Tacoma (1)	Jackson (9)	High Desert (7)	Clinton (4)
St. Louis	Memphis (2)	Springfield (1)	Palm Beach (20)	Peoria (1)
Tampa Bay	Durham (4)	Montgomery (3)	Charlotte (6)	Bowling Green (10)
Texas	Round Rock (1)	Frisco (1)	Myrtle Beach (4)	Hickory (18)
Toronto	Buffalo (1)	New Hampshire (10)	Dunedin (10)	Lansing (3)
Washington	Syracuse (5)	Harrisburg (3)	Potomac (1)	Hagerstown (1)

"Oriole Way" can proceed with low travel costs. But the 1,540 miles that lie between Angel Stadium of Anaheim and the home of the Burlington Bees—Community Stadium in Burlington, Iowa—creates a setting whereby the cost of traveling to check on player development may be a binding constraint on management. Clearly, the Orioles coaching staff and front-office personnel will have an easier time checking personally on the progress of the players in their Class A-level affiliate than the Angels will, all else equal. West coast teams like the Angels, therefore, likely base their travel decisions between Los Angeles and their affiliate in Class A on airline fares and schedules, introducing an affiliate alignment parameter that is beyond the scope of our brief look into regionalization. Nevertheless, these are parameters that matter to enough Major League teams and cannot be ignored when assessing the success of the broader goal to regionalize minor league affiliations, but should be addressed in future research.

Class A Advanced Affiliations and Proximity

Aligning Major League teams with Class A Advanced level affiliates presents some difficulties because of the regional nature of the leagues at this level. There are three leagues at the Class A Advanced level of minor league baseball—the California League, the Carolina League, and the Florida State League. True to the name of two of the leagues at the Class A Advanced, the California League has teams located solely in the state of California, and the Florida State League has teams based only in the state of Florida. The Carolina League has teams stretching outside of North Carolina and South Carolina; teams from the Carolina League are found in Delaware, Maryland, and Virginia in addition to the Carolinas. In all, there are just seven states that are home to the 30 teams in the Class A Advanced level of minor league baseball. Compared to the 17 states, the District of Columbia and Canada where the 30 Major League Baseball teams are located, Class A Advanced-level baseball is much more limited in its geographic reach throughout the US than any other professional baseball league in affiliated baseball. This, of course, limits the opportunity for many Major League teams to be close in geographic proximity to their Class A Advanced affiliate.

With this unique geographical feature in mind, we turn our attention now to a brief examination of how alignment in the Class A Advanced level of the minor leagues has changed since 2003. Approaching the issue of affiliation proximity between Major League teams and Class A Advanced-level teams in the same manner as we did with Class A-level teams, we can make a few quick observations. First, from 2003 to 2013, there was an increase from four to five of the number of Major League teams that were affiliates with the closest minor league team at the Class A Advanced level. Note that this number has not changed since 2005. Additionally, there are now three Major League teams that are within 175 miles of their Class A Advanced-level affiliate even though these teams are not the closest to the Major League team at that particular level. This is an increase from just one Major League team that was within 175 miles of its Class A Advanced-level affiliate in 2003.

One of the unique features of minor league baseball at the Class A Advanced level is that many of the teams that are in the Florida State League play in the same facilities the parent club plays in during spring training. Recall earlier in this chapter our discussion about the St. Louis Cardinals organization and the alignment of their minor league affiliates. While they were affiliated with either the closest or second closest minor league team at three of the four top levels of affiliated minor league baseball, their Class A Advanced-level affiliate was nearly 1,000 miles away from St. Louis; not more than ten minor league teams at that level were further away than the Palm Beach Cardinals.

The St. Louis Cardinals, in fact, are not the only Major League team that is affiliated in this fashion with a team in the Florida State League. In all, 10 of the 12 teams in the Florida State League play in stadiums that also serve as the spring training home for their affiliate Major League parent club. And one more Florida State League team, the Brevard County Manatees, plays in a facility that is also the spring training home to the Washington Nationals, even though the Manatees are the Class A Advanced-level affiliate of the Milwaukee Brewers. Only the Daytona Cubs, Class A Advanced-level affiliate for the Chicago Cubs until 2014, did not play in a stadium that serves as a facility for spring training.

In observing these affiliations, it would seem that enforcing player development strategies matters. In all, ten Major League Baseball teams take advantage of the opportunity to have one facility serve a dual purpose. That is, one facility is used to get the Major League squad ready for the regular season before being used to develop players at the Class A Advanced level during the regular season.[8] This structural dynamic suggests that Major League Baseball teams can enforce player development in a manner that is not simply dependent on proximity to the stadium. For those Major League teams whose Class A Advanced-level affiliate plays at the same facility as they use for spring training, player development can occur in a facility that is Major League quality. All else equal, this should allow players to develop in a manner that is best for the Major League team.

It needs to be noted that the eight Major League teams not located in Florida but having affiliate teams at the Class A Advanced level in the Florida State League appear to have aligned their affiliation to take advantage of the spring training connection. These eight Major League teams are Detroit, Minnesota, both New York teams, Philadelphia, Pittsburgh, St. Louis, and Toronto. There are some data points that suggest this is the case. First, over half of the 13 Major League Baseball teams

[8] Also, it should be noted that this sharing of facilities between spring training use and regular season use occurs even more at lower levels of professional affiliated baseball. The Gulf Coast League in Florida and the Arizona League—Rookie Level baseball—operate a season of approximately 60 games during the summer that further extends the use of the facility for the Major League team. Since we are keeping our focus in this book to minor league baseball at the Class A level and above, we will not address this issue further.

that have maintained affiliations with just one Class A Advanced-level baseball team since 2003 are teams not located in Florida, but with an affiliate playing in the same facility as their spring training home in Florida. Maintaining a relationship with one minor league team over this stretch of time suggests that the Major League team is satisfied with the player development.

Second, across all 30 teams, the average distance between a Major League team and its Class A Advanced-level affiliate is 680 miles. But restricting our attention to just the eight Major League teams not located in Florida and having an affiliate in the Florida State League playing at the same spring training facility as the parent club, the average distance is 1,043 miles. The remaining 22 Major League teams are an average distance of 548 miles from their Class A Advanced-level affiliate. There are costs to the Major League team being further away from the minor league affiliate. But these costs appear to be offset by the benefit of Major League quality facilities at the Class A Advanced level.

Finally, the eight Major League teams not located in Florida that have affiliates playing at their spring training facility in Florida have an average of about 14 other minor league teams that are closer to them at that level. For the rest of the Major League teams (including those located in Florida), there are about eight minor league teams at the Class A Advanced level that are closer than their current affiliate. Because there are more teams available to choose from that are in closer proximity for those teams having affiliates at their spring training facility, it would appear that Major League-quality player development facilities have a benefit that likely offsets the cost of being further away from the parent club.

The evidence from the alignment of these Major League teams with affiliates in the Florida State League points to the existence of a strategy for player development that incorporates more than just proximity to the minor league affiliate as the critical decision-making calculus. Without trying to generalize too much, the evidence appears to point to a decision on the part of the eight Major League teams to locate their Class A Advanced-level teams in the Florida State League playing at the team's spring training facilities. The median proximity ranking for the other three levels of minor league baseball affiliates for these eight teams is either two or three, whereas the median proximity ranking for the Class A Advanced level is 15. This means that the median Major League Baseball team not in Florida but with their Class A Advanced-level affiliate in the Florida State League playing at their spring training facilities are currently an affiliate with the second or third closest team at each of the other levels of affiliated baseball we focus on in this book.

Providing access to the highest quality facility for the purpose of player development seems to be a benefit that Major League teams are willing to pay for in the form of decreased proximity to the minor league affiliate. But this behavior begs the following question: If Major League teams seem to be willing to pay for better quality player development facilities, why don't they pay for them at every level of their minor league system. The most obvious answer is that they don't pay for them because they don't have to. Their monopoly power allows them to exert pressure on their affiliate minor league teams to pay for enhancing the quality of the player development facilities. We only need to return to the story we highlighted at the start of this chapter with the Washington Nationals and their Class A-level affiliate, the Hagerstown Suns. Probably the main reason the Suns are planning to move to Fredericksburg, Virginia, is because they received pressure from the Nationals to enhance the quality of the player development facilities. And it is important to note the lack of funding coming from the Nationals in this move. Once again, this points to the power that Major League Baseball teams have in the minor league baseball arena.

Double A Affiliations and Proximity

There are three leagues at the Double A level of affiliated baseball. The Eastern League has 12 teams, whose teams are spread throughout nine states, while the Southern League has ten teams located in four states. Unlike the California League and Florida State League in Class A Advanced-level baseball whose teams are all located in their league's namesake state, half of the Texas League's eight teams are based in Arkansas, Missouri, and Oklahoma. In all, 17 states have at least one baseball team at the Double A level of the minor leagues. Except for Major League teams in the upper Midwest and in the western half of the US, this provides a decent overlap of the geographic regions covered by Major League Baseball and Double A-level minor league baseball. We now turn our attention to considering how this overlap has impacted the alignment of affiliations at the Double A level.

By some measures, the least amount of change in the overall alignment from 2003 to 2013 of affiliations at the minor league level was at the Double A level. In 2003 eight Major League teams were affiliated with the closest minor league team at the Double A level and five more Major League teams were affiliated with a team at the Double A level that was not the closest at that level but was within 175 miles of the Major League team. In 2013, there were two additional Major League teams that were affiliated with the closest team at the Double A level, giving a total of ten Major League teams that were affiliated with the Double A team closest to them. In total, half of the 30 Major League teams in 2013 were affiliated with a Double A team that was either the closest or within 175 miles of the Major League team.

The lack of change in affiliations described above is partly a function of the change in affiliations occurring in the years leading up to 2003. If we push the starting point of our examination of affiliation proximity back to 1999—the most recent year when each Major League team had one and only one affiliate at the Double A level—we will observe a more obvious move towards affiliations with minor league teams that are closer to the Major League team. In 1999, there were just four Major League teams affiliated with the minor league team at the Double A level closest to them. This number increased to ten in 2013.

What is perhaps more suggestive of a push at this level towards regionalization is that fully 16 Major League teams were affiliated with the same minor league team at the Double A level in 2013 as they were in 2003, and 12 of those 16 Major League teams have affiliations with the minor league team closest to them at the

Double A level or within 175 miles of them. This consistency in affiliation after the flurry of affiliation switches leading up to 2003 suggests a concerted effort on the part of Major League teams to align their affiliations to those teams that are close in proximity. The benefits that can accrue from lower travel costs leading to Major League coaches and front-office personnel having more opportunities to personally check on player development therefore appear to be real.

Triple A Affiliations and Proximity

There are two minor leagues operating at the Triple A level of affiliated baseball. The International League has 14 teams that play in ten states. Not one team has their home stadium outside the US. The Pacific Coast League has 16 teams that play in 13 states. Nearly half these teams play in home stadiums that are closer to a US coastline that is not the Pacific coast. Poor naming of the leagues aside, the Triple A level of minor league baseball is the highest level of professional baseball below Major League Baseball.

Minor league baseball teams at the Triple A level are among the closest to their Major League affiliate as any level in the minor leagues. The average Major League Baseball team is located 350 miles from its minor league affiliate at the Triple A level, making Triple A baseball teams at least half the distance, on average, from their Major League affiliate as compared to any of the other minor league levels. There are at least three obvious reasons why Triple A teams are relatively close to their Major League affiliates. First, Triple A-level affiliates are theoretically the final step in a professional baseball player's development at the minor league level before being called up to the Major League parent club. Many times, the call-up to the majors is planned out and occurs in a manner that is intended to be a natural continuation of player development. These call-ups usually include enough notice so that travel costs involved with bringing the player to the Major League team can be kept to a minimum. Consider the Washington Nationals Stephen Strasburg, who made his Major League debut on June 8, 2010, in Washington against the lowly (at the time) Pittsburgh Pirates. He was called up from the Triple A affiliate Syracuse Chiefs, and arrived in Washington in between scheduled starts. Strasburg's winning performance at home that evening was highlighted by 14 strikeouts over seven innings and helped generate even more attention for the 2009 number one draft pick.

At other times, the call-up to the Major League club is time sensitive. That is, players are called up to fill a roster spot on the Major League team that has been vacated due to an injury. Getting the player to the Major League parent club sooner, rather than later, can be done if the Triple A affiliate is closer to the Major League team. But proximity to the Triple A-level affiliate for this purpose is not a foolproof way to cut down on travel time and costs. Injuries can occur at any time, and neither the Major League club nor its Triple A affiliate plays every game at home. So there could be an occasion when the call-up is at a time when travel distances are longer than expected. For example, when the 2010 number one draft pick Bryce Harper was called up to the Washington Nationals for his Major League debut on April 28, 2012, he had to take a cross-country flight from New York, where he was a member of the Triple A affiliate Syracuse Chiefs, to Los Angeles, where the Nationals were playing the Dodgers.

In both of the above stories highlighting the Washington Nationals top minor league prospects getting called up from the Triple A affiliate, travel costs were likely not a major constraint in the final decision-making process. In one instance, the emergency nature of the call-up necessitated immediate travel plans be made for Bryce Harper. In the other situation, Stephen Strasburg was brought to Washington in between his starts and his debut was likely selected weeks ahead of time. So while theoretically feasible, keeping the cost of player call-ups as low as possible is likely not the only reason Major League teams are relatively close in proximity to their Triple A affiliate.

There is likely another reason why Triple A-level baseball teams are closer, on average, to their Major League affiliate. Rule 58 of the Major League Rules recommends that Triple A stadiums have a seating capacity of 10,000. Most often, a stadium of this size will be located in a metropolitan area that can generate enough fans to fill the stadium just about any given day. These stadiums, and the teams that play in them, can be in a city large enough to be the home of a sports team in one of the other major professional team sports leagues—the National Football League, the National Basketball Association, or the National Hockey League. The stadiums could also be located a short distance from a major metropolitan area that has most of the major professional team sports, including a Major League Baseball team. These areas are generally too small to have two Major League Baseball teams (like New York, Chicago, or Los Angeles) but big enough to be home to an additional professional baseball team at the Triple A level.

An example of the first instance described above is the Columbus Clippers, located in the same city as the National Hockey League's Columbus Bluejackets. Some would note that the Ohio State University football and basketball teams, who also play in Columbus, are big-time enough to be close to professional-quality sports teams. But there is no Major League Baseball team in Columbus, Ohio. So the Columbus Clippers are the highest level of professional baseball in the area. Other cities with a Triple A baseball team and at least one other major professional sports team that fit in this model are Indianapolis, New Orleans, and Salt Lake City. Each of these cities is typically found in lists of possible Major League Baseball expansion cities because of their city size and the fact that they already support another major professional sports team.

The other typical setting for a Triple A baseball team is to be located within a short drive of a major metropolitan area. Examples of this include the Colorado Springs Sky Sox, the Pawtucket Red Sox, the Gwinnett Braves, and the Lehigh Valley Iron Pigs. Each of these teams is just a short drive from their Major League affiliate—respectively, Denver, Boston, Atlanta, and Philadelphia—but they are located in a town or city that is generally not considered to be capable of supporting a team from one of the major professional sports leagues. However, their proximity to the major metropolitan area that is home to their Major League affiliate allows the

Triple A-level team to draw enough fans to potentially fill the approximately 10,000-seat stadium any given day. These settings, then, tell a story suggesting that the metropolitan areas most likely to be home to a Triple A-level baseball team will be relatively close to those areas that are home to Major League Baseball teams. The demographics are structured to make proximity easier to achieve at the Triple A level than at any other level. Simply put, cities that are conducive for a Triple A team to play in are closer in size to Major League cities than any other level of minor league baseball.

As we did with Class A and Double A levels of minor league baseball, we now take a closer look at how regionalization of Triple A-level affiliates has progressed since 2003. The 30 current Major League Baseball teams have been affiliated with one and only one minor league team at the Triple A level since Major League Baseball expanded to the current 30 teams in 1998. In fact, each Major League Baseball team has been affiliated with exactly one minor league team at the Triple A level for at least 35 years, which was when the Seattle Mariners and Toronto Blue Jays were in their first year of expansion play. This is the longest stretch of affiliations like this and suggests the high level of importance a Triple A-level affiliate brings to the Major League team for the purposes of player development.

In 2003, nine Major League teams were affiliates with the Triple A-level team closest to them and three more Major League teams were affiliates with teams close—that is, within 175 miles—to them. By 2013, these numbers increased only slightly, as 11 Major League teams were affiliated with the Triple A team closest to them and four were close. So, Major League teams increased the number of affiliates at the Triple A level that were either close or the closest from 12 to 15 in the years 2003–2013.

Proximity and Affiliations for Major League Baseball

Since 2003, more Major League Baseball teams now have affiliates in the minor leagues that are in closer proximity than before. There are numerous benefits from having these minor league affiliates closer to the Major League parent club—closer tabs can be kept on player development, marketing and branding strategies can be strengthened, and player call-ups can be done faster and cheaper. It appears to be a concerted effort on the part of Major League teams to align with minor league teams that are closer to them because every level of minor league baseball is becoming aligned more regionally now. In 2003, the 30 Major League Baseball teams were affiliated with a total of 120 teams at the Triple A, Double A, Class A Advanced, and Class A levels of minor league baseball. In all, 39 of the 120 affiliations aligned the Major League team with the minor league team that was either the closest at that level or within 175 miles of the Major League club. By 2013, there were 50 affiliations of the 120 possible that were structured as either the closest or close, representing a 28 % increase in the number of affiliations that are considered regional in nature.

We assume in this book that proximity of the minor league affiliate to the Major League parent club is an important feature of the affiliation decision. Of course, there are other reasons besides proximity for a Major League team to want to affiliate with a particular minor league team—past franchise movement, history, league-specific peculiarities at the minor league level, branding and marketing in a different region, and tastes and preferences are just a few of the other features of the affiliation decision that must be considered. But if each minor league baseball team was the closest at their level to only one Major League Baseball team, there would be no proximity concerns in aligning the affiliations among the teams in affiliated baseball. The monopoly power of Major League Baseball teams would likely dictate an alignment of minor league affiliations that were based on proximity alone.

But that is not the setting that we find for professional baseball. Instead, quite a few minor league baseball teams find themselves to be the closest team at their level to more than one Major League Baseball team. And this creates difficulties with aligning affiliations based primarily on proximity. The decision of any one of the 30 Major League teams that needs to be affiliated with exactly one minor league team at each of the four levels of professional baseball from the Class A level and up sometimes depends in part on the actions of other Major League Baseball teams. The complexity of aligning these affiliations across all Major League teams where proximity to the minor league team is a primary feature points to some of the possible benefits from Major League Baseball's monopoly power. Namely, allowing one party involved in the affiliation alignment process—the Major League Baseball team and not the minor league baseball team—to take the primary role in facilitating the affiliations can be a cost-effective strategy. We take some time now to examine the complexity involved in aligning just one Major League team's affiliation at just one level of minor league baseball.

Case Study: A Triple A Affiliate for the Pittsburgh Pirates

As an example of how complex aligning an affiliation can be, we will look more carefully at the Pittsburgh Pirates affiliation with the Indianapolis Indians in the International League. The Indians are the closest minor league team at the Triple A level for four Major League teams—the Chicago Cubs, the Chicago White Sox, the Milwaukee Brewers, and the St. Louis Cardinals. Indianapolis is not the affiliate for any of those four teams, but instead is the Triple A affiliate for the Pittsburgh Pirates, whose closest minor league team at that level is the Columbus Clippers, again in the International League. Note that Pittsburgh is over 300 miles away from Indianapolis, while it is only 162 miles from Columbus. Using the definition of proximity we have established in this chapter, Columbus is close to Pittsburgh because it is less than 175 miles away. Additionally, note that Chicago, Milwaukee, and St. Louis are all closer to Indianapolis than Pittsburgh is by at least 100 miles.

So if Columbus is the closest Triple A-level team to Pittsburgh, why is Columbus not the Pittsburgh Triple A affiliate? Actually, a better question would be to ask why there are fully nine minor league teams at the Triple A level that are closer to Pittsburgh than Indianapolis but are not affiliates with Pittsburgh. The answer to the first question has roots that stretch in part as far away as the Detroit affiliation with the Toledo Mud Hens. The answer to the second question is much more complicated and stretches even further away. By taking a closer look at all the possibilities and implications of aligning affiliations in just the Pittsburgh situation, we can gain insight into the coordination difficulties that are present for many Major League teams as they attempt to align affiliates with minor league teams while making proximity a primary concern. The end result is that aligning affiliations across all levels of minor league baseball is an incredibly difficult process, but the complexities would grow even more without Major League Baseball's monopoly power. We will look at the complexities of aligning affiliates under the current setting now and provide some suggestions as to why Major League Baseball's monopoly power may make some of the alignment decisions easier.

To answer the question of why Columbus is not the Pittsburgh Triple A affiliate, we need to look first at the Toledo Mud Hens. Toledo is the closest Triple A-level team to both the Cleveland Indians and the Detroit Tigers and has been Detroit's affiliate since 1987. Detroit is only about 50 miles from Toledo, so aligning Detroit and Toledo together as affiliates seems like a natural thing to do. Of course, this left Cleveland without an opportunity to align with Toledo, which is their closest minor league team at the Triple A level. So Cleveland was forced to align with another minor league team at the Triple A level that was further away than Toledo. Currently, the Columbus Clippers are the Triple A affiliate for the Cleveland Indians. Columbus and Cleveland are about 125 miles apart, so the Clippers are a close affiliate as designated in our discussion here. What seems to make sense about this affiliation is that Columbus is the second closest Triple A-level minor league team, after Toledo, to Cleveland. Therefore, after Toledo was off the table to affiliate with Cleveland, the second best option of aligning the affiliation between Cleveland and Columbus occurred.

But all of this information does not help us to understand completely why Columbus is aligned with Cleveland. To get deeper in our understanding of this affiliation alignment complexity, we have to also look at those Major League teams that are close to Columbus. After all, having the Clippers affiliated with Cleveland does no good if there is a Major League team that is even closer to Columbus but is affiliated with another minor league team that is not as close. In fact, the Major League team that is closest to the Columbus Clippers is the Cincinnati Reds. But while the Reds are about 100 miles away from Columbus, there is another Triple A-level minor league baseball team closer to Cincinnati than Columbus. The Louisville Bats in the International League are only about 90 miles from Cincinnati, making them the Reds closest Triple A-level minor league baseball team. And it turns out that Cincinnati is the Major League team that is closest to Louisville.

Because the Reds are affiliated with Louisville, Columbus is able to affiliate with Cleveland. And because Columbus is affiliated with Cleveland, Pittsburgh is forced to align their affiliation at the Triple A level with a team that is not closest to them. But now, we have another concern arise. Namely, why is it that Pittsburgh is aligned

Table 3.5 Case study: Triple A minor league teams close to Pittsburgh Pirates

Minor league team	Distance (in miles) to Pittsburgh	Major league parent team	Distance (in miles) to major league parent team
Columbus	162	Cleveland	125
Buffalo	175	Toronto	60
Toledo	201	Detroit	53
Rochester	223	Minnesota	786
Scranton/Wilkes-Barre	233	New York Yankees	98
Lehigh Valley	241	Philadelphia	52
Syracuse	269	Washington	293
Durham	315	Tampa Bay	610
Norfolk	321	Baltimore	169
Indianapolis	329	Pittsburgh	329

with the Indianapolis Indians when there are eight Triple A-level teams—excluding Columbus—that are closer still. The complexities arise quickly when we begin to consider that every Major League team has to affiliate with one Triple A-level team. We will take a brief look now at why it is that Pittsburgh has to align with an affiliate relatively far away. This story is meant to illustrate some of the limits of aligning affiliates across Major League Baseball. But it is also intended to show some of the benefits that can accrue from Major League Baseball's monopoly power and how it allows for a first mover advantage.

After Columbus, there are eight other minor league teams at the Triple A level that are closer to Pittsburgh than Indianapolis. These teams are listed in Table 3.5. We will look at each one of these eight teams in turn, from closest to farthest away, and note which Major League team is affiliated with them. We will also note the proximity rankings for each of these affiliations. It will become clear rather quickly just how complex of a problem aligning affiliations becomes across 30 Major League teams.

The Buffalo Bisons are currently Toronto's Triple A-level affiliate and are the Triple A-level team second closest to Pittsburgh. The Bisons are located about 175 miles from Pittsburgh, but are only 60 miles from the Blue Jays stadium and they are the minor league team at the Triple A level that is closest to Toronto. Further, the Major League team closest to Buffalo is the Toronto Blue Jays, so this affiliation seems to be optimal for both teams involved. The Triple A team next closest to Pittsburgh is the Toledo Mud Hens. The Mud Hens, at 201 miles from Pittsburgh, are Detroit's affiliate and are just 53 miles from Tigers Stadium. Toledo is the Triple A team closest to Detroit. Detroit is, likewise, the closest Major League team to Toledo. Again, this affiliation appears to be optimal.

The next closest Triple A team could be the affiliation that makes the most sense to get switched. In 2014, the Rochester (New York) Red Wings were affiliated with the Minnesota Twins. These two teams are almost 800 miles apart, while Pittsburgh and Rochester are 223 miles apart. There are ten Triple A-level minor league baseball teams that are closer to Minnesota than Rochester, one of them being the

Indianapolis Indians. Switching affiliations between Pittsburgh and Minnesota would lead to decreased travel distances for both Major League teams. The Minnesota Twins and Indianapolis Indians are 512 miles apart, so that potential affiliation would be almost 300 miles closer than the current affiliation. The Pittsburgh Pirates and Rochester Red Wings, at 223 miles apart, would be an affiliation that is over 100 miles closer than the current one. Given that the Pirates and the Twins have maintained their current affiliations since 2005 and 2003, respectively, there is potentially something else besides proximity that matters in establishing and keeping an affiliation. Switching affiliations at this point would require a joint effort on the part of both the Pirates and the Twins.

The next two closest Triple A-level minor league teams are not feasible candidates for switching affiliations. The Scranton/Wilkes-Barre RailRiders and Lehigh Valley Iron Pigs are both located in northeast Pennsylvania and are over 200 miles away from Pittsburgh. But the Pennsylvania connection is not enough to link either of these teams to Pittsburgh. Scranton/Wilkes-Barre is affiliated with the New York Yankees, about 100 miles away. And Lehigh Valley is affiliated with the Philadelphia Phillies, about 50 miles away. Lehigh Valley is the closest Triple A-level team to both the Yankees and Phillies, and Scranton/Wilkes-Barre is the second closest Triple A-level team to the Yankees. So it seems that both of these affiliations make sense from a proximity standpoint.

The remaining three minor league teams that are closer to Pittsburgh than the Indianapolis Indians are the Syracuse Chiefs, the Durham Bulls, and the Norfolk Tides. While each of these minor league teams are not the closest at the Triple A level to the Major League teams they are aligned with, they seem to be the most reasonable affiliations available. Proposing a possible affiliation with the Pittsburgh Pirates and any one of these three minor league teams would not be a Pareto improvement, and is thus not suggested. We can look at each of the Major League teams affiliated with the Triple A teams listed above to determine the feasibility of aligning affiliations any other way than the current way.

The Washington Nationals are affiliated with the Triple A Syracuse Chiefs in the International League. Located 293 miles away from the nation's capital and 269 miles from Pittsburgh, the Syracuse Chiefs are about the same distance from both the Pittsburgh Pirates and the Washington Nationals, so from a proximity standpoint, either affiliation would seem to work. The Chiefs are the fifth closest minor league team to Washington at the Triple A level, so there is a potential to improve the proximity alignment of affiliation for the Nationals. But a simple swap of affiliates between Washington and Pittsburgh would not be a Pareto improvement because the distance from Washington to the Indianapolis Indians would increase by about 200–494 miles.

The same type of story holds for a proposed affiliation swap between the Pirates and either the Tampa Bay Rays or the Baltimore Orioles. Again, based on proximity alone, neither one of these affiliation swaps would be a Pareto improvement. While the Pirates would benefit by being closer to a possible minor league affiliate in either Durham or Norfolk, both the Rays and Orioles would be further away than their current affiliations. In fact, the proximity improvement for the Pirates is almost negligible—about 10 miles closer to Norfolk than Indianapolis and about 15 miles for Durham. But the Rays are about 850 miles from Indianapolis and about 600 miles from Durham, while Baltimore is about 170 miles from Norfolk and about 500 miles from Indianapolis. A potential affiliation swap between the Pirates and either the Rays or the Orioles would thus significantly increase the distance to affiliate for the Rays or the Orioles while only minimally decreasing the distance to affiliate for the Pirates. Neither option is a Pareto improvement, and so neither option is feasible.

This close examination of the Triple A-level affiliation possibilities for the Pittsburgh Pirates reflects the complexities involved in aligning affiliations between Major League and minor league baseball teams. Assuming that proximity matters and can yield benefits to both teams included in the affiliation, there is a potential affiliation swap between the Pirates and the Minnesota Twins that is a Pareto improvement in terms of proximity alone. Of course, there are more variables involved in making an affiliation work between a Major League team and any minor league baseball team than just distance between the two teams. Travel is not only by automobile; air travel is likely for those teams that are more than about 200 miles from their minor league affiliate. And the market price for airline travel between the two cities may differ inversely to terrestrial distance because of supply or demand characteristics that are not addressed in our simple examination. Nevertheless, any attempt to change the distance between the Major League team and its minor league affiliate at any level must involve either a joint move by at least one other Major League team or a move by the currently affiliated minor league team to a location that is closer to the Major League team than the current location.

Chapter 4 takes some of the lessons learned from this cursory look at aligning affiliations between Major League Baseball teams and minor league baseball teams to develop another affiliation allocation model. Proximity between the Major League Baseball team and the minor league team to accomplish the purpose of optimally developing players for the Major League Baseball team is certainly an important piece in determining an allocation of affiliations at each level of minor league baseball. We turn our attention now to developing an algorithm that assigns each minor league baseball team to a unique Major League Baseball team where proximity is the primary factor in how affiliations are determined.

Chapter 4
Another Affiliation Allocation Model

In Chapter 3, we examined what appears to be a trend in Major League Baseball to affiliate with minor league teams that are closer in proximity to the parent club. And while the reasons are somewhat clear for this regionalization push in affiliations across Major League Baseball, the reality is that it is not always easy to coordinate or direct this regionalization effort. With the simple understanding that each of the 30 Major League Baseball teams has one and only one minor league affiliate at each of the four highest levels of minor league baseball, any change in affiliation for one Major League Baseball team at any minor league level must be accompanied by a change for at least one other Major League team at that same level. While any changes in affiliation can occur in a decentralized setting, there are potentially some advantages from coordinating affiliation switches through a central organizing agency. This chapter focuses mainly on those benefits that can come from a more centralized and systematic approach to lining up affiliations between Major League Baseball teams and minor league teams. One of the outcomes of this approach is to suggest a couple of different affiliation schemes that could result in a fair number of Major League Baseball teams being located closer to their minor league affiliates.

Three Benefits of Close Affiliation Proximity

To start, I want to highlight three of the clear benefits of a Major League Baseball team being in closer proximity to any, and perhaps all, of its minor league affiliates. First, enforcement of player development is more likely to occur optimally with minor league affiliates in closer proximity to the Major League parent team. Second, rehab assignments are more likely to be made in an ex ante optimal fashion when minor league affiliates are located close to the Major League team. Finally, minor league affiliates at the various levels within the organization are more likely to be closer to each other if they are close to the Major League parent team, allowing player promotions from one minor league level to the next to be optimally made.

© Springer Science+Business Media New York 2015
T.A. Rhoads, *The Call Up to the Majors*, Sports Economics, Management and Policy 7, DOI 10.1007/978-1-4614-8924-5_4

In all, the three benefits highlighted here focus on optimal player development that is intended to put the best players on the field at the Major League level of the organization. I will examine each of these three benefits of close proximity in the remainder of this section.

First, player development is likely to be a goal that players, coaches, and front-office personnel can realize more easily as geographic distance is diminished and enforcement of a consistent team development philosophy is less costly. More opportunities become available to visit the minor league team when the two teams are in closer proximity to each other. As was highlighted in Chapter 3, the Cardinal Way and Oriole Way are just two examples of how Major League Baseball teams attempt to instill a consistent player development philosophy throughout the organization.

All else equal, the costs of travel between teams are lower when those teams are in closer proximity, so it is possible for the coaches and front-office personnel from the Major League team to make more trips to the minor league facility where the affiliate team plays. And more "face time" between front-office personnel, coaches, and players in the minor league system should be expected to lead to player development strategies being implemented consistently throughout the system. Lower enforcement costs allow player development to progress in an optimal fashion. Affiliate minor league baseball teams located in closer proximity to the Major League team are thus more likely to aid in the optimal player development strategy being implemented, making close proximity to the minor league affiliate preferable for the Major League team.

Second, rehab assignments that are optimally designed and optimally timed for the Major League player to return after a stint on the disabled list can potentially take place at a lower cost when teams are closer to each other. This includes starting the rehab assignment on the optimal day and making it last for an optimal number of games in order to bring the Major League player back up to peak performance as he comes off the disabled list. An optimal rehab assignment also includes placing the Major League player at the proper level of minor league play in order to rehab optimally. While there is no rigid standard by which Major League players progress through a rehab assignment, having more options rather than less is preferred for a Major League team.

We turn our attention now to a few recent examples of some rehab assignments that provide insight into how Major League teams with multiple minor league affiliates in relatively close proximity design rehab assignments. In doing so, we will observe that travel costs and level of play seem to matter. Our examples will focus on the Baltimore Orioles and the Washington Nationals organizations. Both of these organizations are less than 100 miles away from each of their minor league affiliates at the Double A level and below.

For our first example of how proximity to all minor league teams matters when deciding on rehab assignments for a Major League player, consider the Baltimore Orioles relief pitcher Tommy Hunter and his rehab assignment with the Orioles Class A affiliate Delmarva Shorebirds on June 7, 2014. A June 5, 2014, article on MLB.com notes Manager Buck Showalter's comments about the plan for Hunter's rehab assignment: "Saturday he will drive up to Delmarva, it's our only home team [that day]."

The article continues by noting that "Hunter will drive back that night, and the O's will have to make a roster move to add him back prior to Sunday's game."[1] Baltimore is only 89 miles away from Salisbury, Maryland, where the Delmarva Shorebirds are located, so it's a relatively easy 2-h drive between the two stadiums.

Tommy Hunter did drive to Salisbury, Maryland, on June 7, 2014, and he pitched the second inning of the Shorebirds game that evening. He threw 11 pitches, struck out two of the three batters he faced, and hit the other batter, who was then thrown out trying to steal second base. While this type of rehab assignment is not meant to be portrayed as a typical rehab assignment, it is meant to suggest that there is an optimal amount of work for a Major League Baseball player to do in his rehab assignment and an optimal time to take the rehab assignment. Sometimes an optimal rehab assignment is a game or two, and sometimes it is just one inning. And sometimes an optimal rehab assignment is to be scheduled for the day before being reinstated on the Major League team's 25-man roster. But when teams are closer in proximity, it is more likely that the optimal rehab assignment will be done with the least travel impact on the player and his team, which should lead to a better chance of coming back to the Major League team in top playing condition.

Note that manager Buck Showalter's comments highlighted above included an implied reference to the proximity of all of the Orioles minor league affiliates. So while Delmarva was the only Orioles minor league affiliate playing a home game on June 7, Showalter's comment suggests that had another affiliate been playing a home game that day, Tommy Hunter may have pitched at that stadium instead.[2] While Delmarva is much closer to their Major League parent team than most every Class A affiliate—the average distance between a Major League Baseball team and its Class A affiliate is 719 miles—there are two minor league affiliates that are even closer to Baltimore than Delmarva. The Double A-level Bowie Baysox are just 25 miles from Baltimore and the Class A Advanced-level Frederick Keys are 44 miles from Baltimore. It is likely that had either of these teams been playing a home game the same day Tommy Hunter pitched his rehab assignment at Delmarva, the Orioles would have sent him to pitch there instead as the costs of travel would be lower.

The Washington Nationals in May and June 2014 also demonstrated the value of close minor league affiliates in facilitating optimal rehab assignments for their Major League players. Wilson Ramos, the catcher for the Nationals, was on the disabled list twice in the early part of the 2014 season. His first stint on the disabled list lasted from early April until early May. He was then on the disabled list again in mid-June. Each time he came off the disabled list and rejoined the Nationals Major League roster after a rehab assignment that included playing at two different minor league affiliates. Note that each rehab assignment was unique in its length and in its design.

---

[1] Quotes taken from "Hunter to return Sunday, after rehab assignment," accessed June 18, 2014, at http://baltimore.orioles.mlb.com/news/article.jsp?ymd=20140605&content_id=78396184&notebook_id=78414130&vkey=notebook_bal&c_id=bal

[2] Alternatively, the Orioles may have needed to change the date of the rehab assignment to coincide with the date one of their minor league affiliates was playing a home game.

The first rehab assignment for Ramos included playing with the Class A-level Hagerstown Suns in Hagerstown, Maryland, on May 4, 2014, before heading 62 miles to Harrisburg to play for the Double A Harrisburg Senators the next day. Ramos then traveled 96 miles to rejoin the Nationals on May 7, 2014, in a game against the Dodgers. Of note with this rehab assignment was that the Hagerstown Suns played a home game on May 5, but the Nationals sent Ramos to play at Double A Harrisburg on that day. This suggests that the level of play matters in designing an optimal rehab assignment, as Ramos could have remained in Hagerstown for the game on May 5 and could have traveled less between games. Having teams located this close to each other gives the Nationals an opportunity to design a rehab assignment so that the appropriate level of play can properly prepare their Major League player to return to the lineup ready to play at the highest level.

The second rehab assignment for Ramos was from June 20, 2014, to June 23, 2014, giving Ramos a four-game rehab assignment. He played two games with the Double A Harrisburg Senators on June 20–21, 2014, before driving 112 miles to Woodbridge, Virginia, and playing two games with the Class A Advanced Potomac Nationals on June 22–23. While it would have likely been better to remain with Harrisburg for the four games and avoid unnecessary travel, the Nationals were forced to move Ramos to Potomac as Harrisburg's home stand ended on June 22. Potomac and the Class A Hagerstown Suns were both playing home games on June 22–23. And while it was further to drive Ramos to Woodbridge, Virginia, instead of Hagerstown, Maryland (112 miles instead of 62 miles), the Nationals made the decision to rehab Ramos at the Class A Advanced level instead of the Class A level. This suggests an optimal rehab assignment for the Major League player that considers both travel distance and level of play. After coming off the disabled list, Ramos then flew to Chicago to meet up with his Major League team for a series against the Cubs that started on June 26, 2014.

There is a random timing of injuries in Major League Baseball and the rehab assignments associated with those injuries are thus subject to the random timing of those injuries. Having at least one minor league affiliate relatively close to the Major League Baseball team can potentially keep travel costs associated with rehab assignments low. Additionally, more minor league affiliates in relatively close proximity can allow the Major League Baseball player that is soon to come off the disabled list to have an optimally timed rehab assignment at a level best designed to get him ready for play at the highest professional level.

There is a third benefit from having minor league affiliates in close proximity to the Major League parent team that is not quite as obvious as the first two we have already examined. It follows that when more of the minor league affiliates of a Major League team are in close proximity to the parent team, they will likely be in close proximity to each other. This matters when moving players from one level in the organization to the next. Travel costs become lower when, for example, the Double A team is relatively close to the Class A Advanced-level team in the same organization. The Washington Nationals Double A affiliate is the Harrisburg Senators in Harrisburg, Pennsylvania. Promoting a player from the Class A Advanced-level Potomac Nationals in Woodbridge, Virginia, means that player must make a trip of 112 miles—about 2 or 3 h by car—from Woodbridge to Harrisburg. While not necessarily an enviable drive to make on a game day for a minor league player, this kind of proximity between affiliates in the Nationals organization provides the Washington Nationals the opportunity to promote a player from Class A Advanced to Double A without much advance notice. This is especially helpful when an injury to a player on the Nationals makes a promotion necessary. The end result is that Major League teams can make player personnel moves when the opportunity arises without the additional burden of considering the travel time and cost for moving those players across levels.

While the Washington Nationals provide a good example of the possibility to promote players from Class A Advanced to Double A without letting travel time and cost be a constraint, consider instead the Houston Astros organization. Promoting a player from their Class A Advanced-level Lancaster Jethawks in Lancaster, California, to the Double A-level Corpus Christi Hooks in Corpus Christi, Texas, involves a trip for that player of over 1,300 miles. Clearly, this is a distance that cannot easily be covered by car in an afternoon. Promotions due to an injury of a player on the Astros may not be able to occur immediately because of the constraint imposed by the travel distance and costs between Lancaster and Corpus Christi.

Of course, minor league players are not forced to progress in a stepwise fashion from one level to the next. Sometimes, players are able to be promoted by skipping a level. But even this creates some distance constraints for the Astros organization, as there is not less than 1,000 miles between minor league affiliates when skipping one level of the organization. All of this suggests that the Houston Astros organization, and others like it, face non-negligible constraints in moving their minor league players from one level to the next that may lead to a second-best promotion of players. Compared to an organization like the Washington Nationals, this constraint may have an impact at the margin that could influence the development of the players in the organization. In fact, this phenomenon seems like an area for research that has yet to be explored fully.

Having focused our attention here on the benefits of regionalizing minor league affiliates and close geographic proximity to the Major League team, our attention will now turn to the task of developing a metric to determine how close Major League Baseball teams are to their minor league affiliates. This process is not an easy one, as there are many rules and regulations imposed by Major League Baseball regarding the location of teams in relation to Major League and affiliated minor league baseball teams. The existing territorial rules suggest that there are limits to how close any given Major League Baseball team can be to its minor league affiliate at any level. Further restrictions are in place limiting the proximity of affiliated minor league teams from other minor league baseball teams.

But perhaps an even bigger constraint is that affiliations must be made within the structure of a system that does not easily allow minor league baseball teams to move or to change levels. Therefore, working with the existing distribution of Major League and affiliated minor league baseball teams, I will provide detail on how to efficiently allocate the affiliations of minor league baseball teams at each level across Major League Baseball teams. What emerges is a better understanding of the limits to achieving regionalization for the entire league. Additionally, this examination will make it clear that without making some dramatic changes within affiliated baseball, some Major League Baseball teams will always have an organization of affiliated minor league teams that are significantly more dispersed geographically than other Major League Baseball teams. These issues are developed and addressed in the remainder of this chapter.

Efficiency in Allocation of Minor League Affiliations

As noted in the previous chapters, the geographic distance between a Major League Baseball team and its minor league affiliate is an important element in the player development process for all Major League Baseball organizations. We assume that, all else equal, a Major League Baseball team prefers a minor league affiliate that is geographically closer instead of further away for the reasons given in the previous chapter and for the reasons expanded on earlier in this chapter. Note that prior research by Gitter and Rhoads (2010) suggests that Major League Baseball games can serve as a substitute for minor league baseball games and lead to fewer fans attending minor league baseball games. There is enough evidence to suggest that minor league baseball teams would not prefer to be located too close to any Major League Baseball team if there was only the negative impact that proximity has on attendance at the minor league team and no positive impact seen from rehab assignments and the desire to see the best prospects progress through the organization.

But Major League Baseball's monopoly power stemming from its antitrust exemption and the subsequent brand value it commands as the only producer of the highest level of professional baseball in the world allow Major League Baseball teams to hold the decided power advantage in dictating the terms of affiliations in the Player Development Contracts that bind Major League teams with their minor league affiliates. As a result, we assume that Major League Baseball teams prefer closer proximity to all of their minor league affiliates, all else equal, and can enter into agreements with minor league teams that allow this to happen. This assumption provides a simplifying element to our algorithm used to generate an efficient allocation of minor league affiliates at each of the four highest levels of affiliated minor league baseball.

Throughout the rest of this chapter, I will develop a simple method that is intended to generate a Pareto efficient allocation of minor league affiliations for all Major League Baseball teams at the Class A level up through the Triple A level. Pareto efficiency is a concept that is often used by economists to assess an allocation of resources among a number of different agents. Often used in designing public policy, Pareto efficient policies are designed not as much for optimizing wealth or utility, for example, but instead they are intended to create a focal point that is easily understood and can be tested or verified. Pareto efficiency in the design of any government policy is meant to provide an allocation of resources—through tax breaks or subsidies, for example—where no agent can be made better off without at least one agent being made worse off. In other words, deviation from a Pareto efficient policy will necessarily mean that at least one agent is worse off than before. Setting this as the determining criteria for the evaluation of the merits of a policy sets a bar that does not unilaterally lead to the most wealth or the highest level of utility being generated, but it is a metric that is nonetheless meaningful in its interpretation.

A Pareto efficient allocation of affiliated minor league baseball teams suggests that the assignment of minor league teams to a parent Major League Baseball team is made in such a way that no improvement in affiliation allocation exists where the distance between the minor league team and a potential parent Major League Baseball team could be decreased without making at least one other Major League Baseball team worse off by being affiliated with a minor league team that is further away than before. That is, the aggregate distance between Major League Baseball teams and their minor league affiliate at a particular level cannot be decreased without at least one Major League Baseball team having its affiliated minor league team located further away.

Pareto efficiency is used as a determining mechanism in the allocation of affiliations between Major League and minor league baseball teams because of the unique nature of affiliated baseball in North America. Specifically, there are 30 Major League Baseball teams that each has one and only one affiliate at each level of minor league baseball. Switching the affiliation for any one Major League Baseball team must, by design, lead to switching the affiliation of at least one other Major League Baseball team. Understanding the reality and the constraints within which these affiliations are determined suggests that any deviation from a Pareto efficient allocation of minor league affiliates will leave at least one Major League Baseball team with an affiliate minor league team that is located further away. Assuming that this is not desired and defining it as a loss of welfare for the Major League team that would be further away from its affiliate, the Pareto efficient allocation is a natural standard we can propose that allows thoughtful and measurable comparisons to the current affiliations and any proposed changes in those affiliations. It is with this Pareto efficient standard that we begin our analysis of minor league affiliations.

Determining a Pareto Efficient Affiliation Allocation

In this section, I describe the procedure by which I arrive at a Pareto efficient allocation of affiliations for each level of minor league baseball. I must note at least two things about the Pareto efficient affiliation pairs that I am proposing here. First, there are multiple allocations of Pareto efficient affiliate pairs that can be constructed with the current geographic distribution of Major League and minor league baseball teams. The Pareto efficient allocation I will propose here puts a premium on matching up a Major League team with the closest available minor league team at each level. That is, closest proximity to the Major League team—proximity rank—matters most in developing this algorithm. The second thing to note about the Pareto efficient affiliate pairs I am proposing here is that focusing on proximity rank may not always lead to the lowest aggregate miles between affiliate pairs across all of Major League Baseball. Instead, the Pareto efficient allocation of affiliations simply provides a distribution of minor league teams to Major League teams from which no deviation can be made without making at least one Major League Baseball team further away from their assigned affiliate minor league team. In Chapter 5, I will offer some policy suggestions regarding affiliation pairs that attempt to improve upon the Pareto efficient allocation where proximity rank matters most.

In implementing the affiliate allocation algorithm, it is assumed that Major League Baseball teams have a preference to be affiliated with the closest available minor league baseball team. The term "available" will become clearer when the allocation procedure is described in detail below. To begin, understand that the process of assigning affiliate pairs would be simplified tremendously if the actual geographic distribution of teams was such that (1) each Major League team was uniquely closest to one and only one minor league team and (2) each minor league team was uniquely closest to one and only one Major League team which is the same Major League team in (1) above. Unfortunately, this is not the case with the current distribution of Major League and minor league teams. While there are some affiliate pairs that emerge in the manner described above—that is, where the Major League team's closest minor league team has that same Major League team as its closest Major League team—it is more likely that one minor league team is the closest at a particular level to multiple Major League teams. We will look at a couple of examples of how Pareto efficient affiliate pairs are determined before describing the algorithm used to generate the Pareto efficient allocation of affiliates. One example is a simple case, and the other example is slightly more complex.

Before continuing, we need to highlight how the data was collected for determining distance data and Pareto efficient affiliate pairs. For all distance calculations throughout this chapter and the rest of this book, I entered the zip codes of the address of each baseball team provided in the 2014 Baseball America Directory into the zip code distance calculator on www.zip-codes.com. The affiliations in place in 2014 are treated as the current affiliations.[3] Two distances are provided through this online distance calculator. The first is the direct line distance which uses the latitude and longitude map coordinates to calculate distance between the two zip code locations. The second distance provided is the driving distance between the two zip code locations. For all of the distance calculations used in this book, the direct line distance between the two cities is used. While this does not necessarily represent the actual travel distance, it is assumed that there is not enough difference between direct line distance and travel distance to alter the results significantly and any differences are likely to be consistent across locational pairs. Additionally, driving distance is only helpful for those potential locational pairs that are close enough to drive and not fly. Typically, that distance is not more than 200 miles. So once a large enough distance is reached between two locations, direct line distance more closely estimates travel distance than driving distance because it more closely estimates travel by air instead of travel by car.

[3] Affiliations between some Major League Baseball teams and some minor league baseball teams changed in October 2014. Some, but not all, of these new affiliations are discussed in Chapter 5.

In our first example we will look at how to determine that the Boston Red Sox and the Triple A-level Pawtucket Red Sox are a Pareto efficient affiliation pair. The closest minor league team at the Triple A level to the Boston Red Sox is the Pawtucket Red Sox and the closest Major League team to the Pawtucket Red Sox is the Boston Red Sox. These teams are just 35 miles apart and no Major League or minor league teams are located in between Boston and Pawtucket. Further, no other Major League teams can claim Pawtucket as the closest Triple A-level minor league team and no other Triple A-level minor league team can claim Boston as the closest Major League team. Therefore, an allocation of affiliations that includes Pawtucket as an affiliate of the Boston Red Sox is Pareto efficient because any switch away from Pawtucket would mean that Boston's minor league affiliate would be further away, which is assumed to be a decrease in utility for the Boston Red Sox. Note that in determining Pareto efficiency, the utility for the Pawtucket Red Sox is not considered.

The example above with Boston and Pawtucket demonstrates a simple determination of a Pareto efficient affiliate pair. Alternatively, consider the following example of determining affiliate pairs at the Class A Advanced level for the Oakland A's and the San Francisco Giants. We will show in this example that simply finding the minor league team closest to each Major League team does not lead to an unambiguous determination of Pareto efficient affiliate pairs for all of Major League Baseball. The San Jose Giants are the closest minor league team for both Oakland and San Francisco. But only one Major League team can have San Jose as their affiliate minor league team at the Class A Advanced level.[4] To determine which Major League team is a Pareto efficient affiliate for the San Jose Giants, we need to identify the Major League team closest to San Jose.

Using direct line distance, San Jose is located 33 miles away from Oakland, and 41 miles away from San Francisco. Because the San Jose Giants are closer to Oakland than they are to San Francisco, we can assign the San Jose Giants and the Oakland A's to be a Pareto efficient affiliate pair. It should be clear that any switch away from Oakland and San Jose as an affiliate pair would lead to a greater distance between Oakland and any other newly prescribed minor league affiliate.

Although we have assigned Oakland and San Jose as an affiliate pair at the Class A Advanced level, we must still determine a Pareto efficient affiliate pair for the San Francisco Giants. Now that Oakland has been assigned San Jose as an affiliate in our algorithm, we must identify the next closest minor league team to San Francisco since San Jose is no longer an available minor league team. The Stockton Ports are located 59 miles away from San Francisco. But Stockton is additionally the closest Class A Advanced-level minor league for the Seattle Mariners. Using the same procedure as above, we determine that the direct line distance between Seattle, Washington, and Stockton, California, is 666 miles. We can assign San Francisco and Stockton as a Pareto efficient affiliate pair.

There are two observations to highlight in establishing the Pareto efficient affiliate pairs with Oakland and San Francisco as we have. First, we could have just as easily assigned San Jose to be the minor league affiliate to the San Francisco Giants and

---

[4] Not all minor leagues have affiliation models like affiliated baseball. Note that NBA D-League teams may have affiliations across more than one NBA team.

Stockton to be the minor league affiliate to the Oakland A's. This alternative assignment would be Pareto efficient—while Oakland would benefit from a switch in affiliations away from Stockton, San Francisco can do no better than an affiliation with San Jose. Note that the current affiliations for both Oakland and San Francisco are the latter ones in this example.[5]

The second observation is that the Pareto efficient affiliate pair of Oakland/San Jose and San Francisco/Stockton has a greater aggregate distance between affiliates (92 miles) than the Oakland/Stockton and San Francisco/San Jose Pareto efficient affiliate pair (91 miles). While the difference in aggregate distance is negligible, it points to one of the limits in designing an allocation of Pareto efficient affiliate pairs where priority is given to the closest Major League Baseball team. Namely, the affiliate pairing algorithm I have designed is not sufficient to generate the minimum sum of distances between affiliate pairs across Major League Baseball. Instead, the fundamental key in the model I have designed to determine a Pareto efficient allocation of affiliate pairs is that maximizing proximity rank—that is, pairing up Major League teams with the closest available minor league team—is of greater importance than minimizing aggregate distance between affiliate pairs across all of Major League Baseball. Designing the affiliate pairing model in this way is better suited to a policy of regionalization in affiliated baseball that we are seeing today. The next section provides the details of how the allocation of Pareto efficient affiliate pairs was determined across all of Major League Baseball for the Class A level and above.

Affiliate Pairing Model Algorithm

We now provide detail on exactly how Pareto efficient affiliate pairs were determined for each level of minor league baseball. Recognizing that numerous Pareto efficient allocations of affiliate pairs exist, we must decide upon the guiding principles and assumptions to use in crafting an allocation that is sound throughout its design and implementation. Our goal is to develop a set of Pareto efficient affiliate pairs here that will serve as an optimal allocation of affiliate pairs for Major League Baseball to attain. Note that this optimal allocation of affiliate pairs is to be interpreted as a theoretical construct, and not an allocation set to be implemented through policy. We will hold until Chapter 5 a set of suggested affiliation switches that can generate a movement towards the Pareto efficient affiliate pairs introduced here but use the current affiliate pairs as a starting point. In other words, our Pareto efficient affiliate pairs developed here frame our policy suggestions for Major League Baseball.

The fundamental assumption underlying this allocation methodology is that affiliate pairs that are closer together are given preference over those that are farther apart from each other. This is, of course, only a concern when multiple Major League Baseball teams can claim the same minor league team as the closest available team.

[5] Notice that the San Jose Giants took the name of their affiliate Major League parent team.

Because there is a one-to-one assignment of Major League and affiliate minor league baseball teams and because there are numerous occasions when multiple Major League teams claim the same minor league team as the closest, our methodology demands this mechanism. The current geographic distribution of Major League and minor league teams is assumed exogenous and fixed. While it may be appealing to consider possible new locations for Major League or minor league baseball teams—for example, Portland, Oregon, is often touted as a prime location for a Major League or minor league baseball team[6]—we will assume that there are too many political and institutional barriers to establishing a new set of cities to serve as host for Major League or minor league baseball teams.

The allocation mechanism used here turns out to be an iterated series of matching a Major League Baseball team with a minor league baseball team for which both teams are each other's closest team at that level. Earlier examples were presented highlighting what an affiliate pair looks like. Of course, the mechanism allowing us to do this for all Major League Baseball teams at each level given the current geographic distribution of teams becomes more complicated than doing it for just a couple of Major League Baseball teams. Determining the affiliation pairs for the Oakland A's and the San Francisco Giants, for example, is a quick exercise that involves no more than two iterations of establishing the closest affiliate pair. But the process for deciding upon 30 affiliation pairs at each of the four highest levels of the minor leagues involves considerably more iterations.

The process of matching up affiliation pairs at each minor league level is structured as follows. We list out the steps in this algorithm that assigns affiliate pairs to all 30 Major League Baseball teams. A sample of the allocation table for the Triple A level is included here to help demonstrate the affiliation pairing allocation mechanism.

A	B	C
MLB Team	Closest MiLB Team	Column B's closest MLB Team
Arizona Diamondbacks	Las Vegas 51s	Los Angeles Angels of Anaheim
Atlanta Braves	Gwinnett Braves	Atlanta Braves
Baltimore Orioles	Lehigh Valley Iron Pigs	Philadelphia Phillies
Boston Red Sox	Pawtucket Red Sox	Boston Red Sox

1. List all the Major League Baseball teams in column A.
2. For each Major League Baseball team, determine the closest minor league team. Include this minor league team in column B.
3. For each minor league team listed in column B, determine the closest Major League Baseball team. List this Major League Baseball team in column C.
4. An affiliate pair exists between a Major League Baseball team in column A and a minor league team in column B if and only if column A and column C include the same Major League Baseball team.

[6] Ringolsby (2014) discusses Portland's status as a possible location for a Major League Baseball team.

5. Remove from the allocation exercise all Major League Baseball teams and minor league baseball teams for which an affiliation pair has been determined using the guidelines listed in step 4 above.
6. Repeat steps 1–5 above with the remaining Major League and minor league teams until all 30 Major League Baseball teams have been paired with exactly one minor league team.

Through the design of the allocation mechanism above and with the unique allocation of affiliate pairs it produces, we can be sure that no Pareto improvement exists when distance between affiliate pair is the metric of interest. It must be noted again that this allocation mechanism is not guaranteed to produce a complete set of affiliation pairs for which aggregate distance between affiliates is minimized. In fact, we will show in Chapter 5 suggestions to switch affiliates away from the current pairings that will yield an aggregate distance between affiliates that is lower than what is determined here. But for now, we introduce this set of affiliate pairs as a Pareto efficient allocation that puts the primary focus on matching up the closest available minor league team to each Major League Baseball team. In this fashion, we effectively are establishing the starting point for making policy suggestions for policy aimed at switching affiliations. In these next sections, we provide the listing of all the affiliate pairs at the four highest levels of minor league baseball. All of these affiliate pairs were derived using the iterated allocation mechanism described above.

Triple A Pareto Efficient Affiliate Pairs

Of the four highest levels of minor league baseball for which these Pareto efficient affiliate pairs are derived, the Triple A level required the fewest rounds of iterated allocation. All 30 Major League Baseball teams were assigned exactly one Triple A affiliate through this mechanism by the fifth round of iterated allocation. There were 13 affiliate pairs determined in the first round of allocations alone, meaning that the current geographic distribution of Triple A teams is generally close to many of the current Major League Baseball teams. Further, 15 Major League teams were matched with their closest Triple A team using this allocation mechanism. Fully half of the Major League teams were paired with the closest Triple A team, suggesting that the allocation mechanism is doing what it is meant to do by pairing up as many Major League Baseball teams as possible to the closest available minor league team.

A major factor in settling on all 30 Pareto efficient affiliate pairs in just five rounds of allocation iterations is that Triple A teams are located in relatively high-population locations. Of course, this means that Triple A teams are located relatively close to cities that likely host a Major League Baseball team. In large measure, this is because the Major League Rules require Triple A stadiums to have a stadium capacity to seat at least 10,000 fans.[7] For the most part, this requirement limits the geographic areas

[7] Attachment 58 of the Major League Rules stipulates stadium capacity of 10,000 for Triple A, 6,000 for Double A, and 4,000 for A-level baseball.

where Triple A teams can be located to those areas within a reasonable distance to major metropolitan areas in the US. To put it another way, it is far less likely that an affiliated minor league baseball team can expect to be profitable in a less populated part of the country that is far away from a metropolitan population center while maintaining a stadium with at least 10,000 seats.

Included here is the allocation table with some explanation of the data. The first column contains the Major League Baseball team and the second column lists the Pareto efficient minor league affiliate. An asterisk next to the affiliate in the Pareto efficient affiliate column indicates that team was the 2014 Triple A affiliate. Note that the Triple A teams listed in parenthesis after some of the Pareto efficient affiliates are the minor league teams that are closer to the Major League team in the first column but were already assigned to another Major League team because of closer proximity. As an example, the Baltimore Orioles Pareto efficient Triple A affiliate in Table 4.1

Table 4.1 Triple A Pareto efficient affiliate pairs

MLB team	PE affiliate (closer Triple A teams)	Distance
Arizona	Albuquerque (Las Vegas)	330
Atlanta	Gwinnett*	29
Baltimore	Durham (Lehigh Valley, Scranton)	260
Boston	Pawtucket*	36
Chicago Cubs	Nashville (Indianapolis)	404
Chicago White Sox	Indianapolis	164
Cincinnati	Louisville*	86
Cleveland	Columbus* (Toledo)	126
Colorado	Colorado Springs*	62
Detroit	Toledo*	54
Houston	Round Rock	147
Kansas City	Omaha*	166
Los Angeles Angels	Las Vegas	224
Los Angeles Dodgers	Reno (Fresno)	387
Miami	Charlotte (Gwinnett)	654
Milwaukee	El Paso (Indianapolis, Nashville)	1,273
Minnesota	Iowa	235
NY Mets	Syracuse (Lehigh Valley, Scranton)	199
NY Yankees	Scranton* (Lehigh Valley)	99
Oakland	Sacramento*	70
Philadelphia	Lehigh Valley*	53
Pittsburgh	Rochester (Columbus)	223
Saint Louis	Memphis* (Indianapolis)	240
San Diego	Salt Lake (Las Vegas, Fresno, Reno)	625
San Francisco	Fresno* (Sacramento)	160
Seattle	Tacoma*	23
Tampa Bay	New Orleans (Gwinnett)	486
Texas	Oklahoma City (Round Rock)	189
Toronto	Buffalo*	60
Washington	Norfolk	145

is Durham as determined by our allocation mechanism. But Lehigh Valley and Scranton are closer minor league teams and are included in parentheses—the Philadelphia Phillies are matched with Lehigh Valley and the New York Yankees are matched with Scranton. Finally, the last column notes the distance, in miles, between each affiliate pair.

The aggregate distance for the 30 affiliate pairs listed above is 7,209 miles and the mean and median distances between a Major League Baseball team in its Triple A Pareto efficient affiliate using our methodology are 240 and 165 miles, respectively. Compare this to the aggregate distance of 10,780 miles for the 30 affiliate pairs in 2014. Recall that we briefly looked at the distance and proximity ranking data of the 2014 affiliations back in Chapter 3. In 2014, the mean and median distances between a Major League Baseball team and its Triple A affiliate are 360 and 205 miles. The Pareto efficient allocation of affiliate pairs therefore cuts the mean distance between affiliates by one-third and cuts the median distance by about one-fifth.

Something to be noted with the allocation mechanism at the Triple A level is that 14 of the affiliate pairs in this Pareto efficient allocation are the same as the 2014 affiliation pairs. The recent push on the part of Major League Baseball towards regionalization of minor league affiliates is likely a major reason that nearly half of the Major League Baseball teams have affiliates that match with this Pareto efficient allocation. Still, there is room to suggest some affiliate swaps that could be Pareto improvements over the allocation scheme that currently exists in Triple A baseball. We will make these suggestions in Chapter 5. We move our attention now to the Double A level.

Double A Pareto Efficient Affiliate Pairs

It took more iterations for the allocation mechanism to arrive at a Pareto efficient allocation of affiliate pairs for the Double A level than it did for Triple A. In fact, Triple A was the only level where the allocation mechanism was able to match affiliate pairs in no more than five iterations. In large measure, minor league baseball teams at levels below Triple A are found in locations with populations far below the major metropolitan areas where Major League Baseball teams are. But this is not the primary reason the allocation mechanism used here goes through many iterations to match affiliate pairs at these lower levels of minor league baseball. Instead, the longer time it takes to match affiliate pairs is largely a function of the regional nature of the leagues at the levels of baseball below Triple A. We will focus our attention now on the regional nature of the three leagues at the Double A level.

Double A baseball is largely centered in the eastern and southeastern parts of the US. The Eastern League's 12 teams are spread across nine states, the Southern League has ten teams in four states, and the Texas League has half of its eight teams in Texas and the rest of the teams in three other states. As a result, many of the Major League Baseball teams located in the upper Midwest and in the Western US are similarly located closest to the same Double A-level teams and this leads to multiple iterations in the allocation mechanism to match affiliate pairs. We will look at two examples to help illustrate this phenomenon.

The first example shows the Midland RockHounds in the Texas League as the closest Double A-level team for seven Major League Baseball teams. All of these teams are in the Western half of the US—the Arizona Diamondbacks, Los Angeles Dodgers, Los Angeles Angels, Oakland A's, San Diego Padres, San Francisco Giants, and Seattle Mariners. Our allocation mechanism assigns Midland to be paired with the Arizona Diamondbacks, but there are actually three Major League teams that are closer to Midland than Arizona. The Texas Rangers, Houston Astros, and Colorado Rockies are all closer to Midland than the Arizona Diamondbacks, but each one of these teams is matched with another minor league affiliate that is closer than Midland. Therefore, it is not until the fourth iteration of the allocation mechanism where Arizona and Midland are matched as an affiliate pair. This leaves the other six Major League teams that claim Midland as the closest Double A-level minor league team again claiming the same team as the next closest. In this case, it is now the San Antonio Missions of the Texas League. As with assigning an affiliate pair for Midland, it likewise takes multiple iterations to assign affiliate pairs to the remaining Major League Baseball teams.

The second example involves the Akron RubberDucks of the Eastern League and six Major League Baseball teams in the upper Midwest. The RubberDucks are matched in the first iteration of the allocation procedure with the Cleveland Indians. This is an affiliate pair that makes sense as Akron is the closest Double A-level team to Cleveland. But the iterative process is extended for five other Major League teams—the Chicago Cubs, Chicago White Sox, Cincinnati Reds, Detroit Tigers, and Milwaukee Brewers—for whom Akron is also the closest Double A-level minor league baseball team. In the second iteration of the allocation mechanism, four of these teams claim the Erie SeaWolves as their closest Double A team after Akron. Again, this leads to an iterative process that takes much longer than if most Major League Baseball teams were uniquely closest to one minor league team.

In total, the Pareto efficient Double A affiliate pairs are matched for all 30 Major League teams after a series of 12 iterations. The first four iterations of the allocation process assigned 22 affiliate pairs. As a comparison, the first four iterations for the Triple A level resulted in assigning 29 affiliate pairs. Note that the each of the last eight iterations at the Double A level only assigned one affiliate pair. Further, with the exception of the Arizona Diamondbacks, all of the Major League Baseball teams involved in the last six iterations of the allocation process were those teams for whom Midland was the closest Double A-level minor league team.

Table 4.2 lists the Double A-level Pareto efficient affiliate pairs for all 30 Major League teams. There are 13 Major League Baseball teams in this list that are matched with their closest Double A-level baseball team. These affiliate pairs are those for which there are no closer Double A teams listed in parentheses in the second column of Table 4.2. Recall that this same iterated allocation mechanism produced 15 Pareto efficient affiliate pairs at the Triple A level that matched a Major League Baseball team with its closest minor league team. So far, the allocation mechanism assigning the affiliate pairs seems to be doing a fairly good job of matching about half of the

Table 4.2 Double A Pareto efficient affiliate pairs

MLB team	PE affiliate (closer Double A teams)	Distance
Arizona	Midland	594
Atlanta	Chattanooga	107
Baltimore	Harrisburg (Bowie)	68
Boston	New Hampshire	48
Chicago Cubs	NW Arkansas (Akron, Erie, Altoona, Jackson, Tennessee, Chattanooga, Huntsville, Springfield)	532
Chicago White Sox	Huntsville (Akron, Erie, Altoona, Jackson, Tennessee, Chattanooga, Springfield)	496
Cincinnati	Tennessee (Akron)	222
Cleveland	Akron*	29
Colorado	Tulsa*	549
Detroit	Reading (Akron, Erie, Altoona, Harrisburg, Binghamton)	392
Houston	Corpus Christi*	183
Kansas City	Springfield	141
Los Angeles Angels	Mississippi (Midland, San Antonio, Corpus Christi, Tulsa, Frisco, Springfield, Northwest Arkansas, Arkansas)	1,607
Los Angeles Dodgers	Mobile (Midland, San Antonio, Corpus Christi, Tulsa, Frisco, Springfield, Northwest Arkansas, Arkansas, Mississippi, Jackson)	1,768
Miami	Pensacola (Jacksonville)	531
Milwaukee	Arkansas (Akron, Erie, Springfield, Jackson, Altoona, Tennessee, Chattanooga, Northwest Arkansas, Huntsville, Harrisburg)	614
Minnesota	Birmingham (more than 10 teams closer)	864
NY Mets	Binghamton* (Trenton, New Britain, Reading)	143
NY Yankees	New Britain (Trenton)	84
Oakland	Montgomery (more than ten teams closer)	2,050
Philadelphia	Trenton	29
Pittsburgh	Altoona*	87
Saint Louis	Jackson (Springfield)	216
San Diego	San Antonio* (Midland)	1,120
San Francisco	Portland (more than ten teams closer)	2,713
Seattle	Richmond (more than ten teams closer)	2,348
Tampa Bay	Jacksonville	188
Texas	Frisco*	30
Toronto	Erie	111
Washington	Bowie	15

Major League Baseball teams with their closest minor league team at the Triple A and Double A levels.

The aggregate distance for our 30 affiliate pairs in Table 4.2 is 17,879 miles. The mean and median distances are 596 and 219 miles, respectively. Compare these distances to those found under the 2014 affiliation scheme. The aggregate distance of the 30 affiliate pairs in 2014 was 18,062 miles and the mean and median distances were 602 and 368 miles, respectively. While the mean affiliate pairing distance only dropped by about 1% using the Pareto efficient iterated allocation mechanism, we were able to cut the median distance by about 40%. This is quite a large decrease in median distance between affiliate pairs and suggests that there is potential for suggesting alternatives to the current allocation of affiliate pairs that exists in Major League Baseball today. Again, we will address these alternatives in Chapter 5.

Class A Advanced Pareto Efficient Affiliate Pairs

Similar to the Double A level of minor league baseball, and as we will also see with the Class A level, the regional nature of the league structure at the Class A Advanced level leads to a large number of iterations in our iterated Pareto efficient affiliate pairing mechanism. Specifically, there are 15 rounds of iterations needed to assign an affiliate pair for all 30 Major League Baseball teams. Contrast this to the five rounds required for the Triple A level and the 12 rounds of iterations needed for the Double A level. In fact, of the four levels of minor league baseball that we examine in this book, the Class A Advanced level requires the most rounds of iterations to assign the affiliate pairs for all of the Major League Baseball teams.

There are three leagues that operate at the Class A Advanced level. The California League and the Florida State League are both true to their name, with all the teams in each respective league based in their namesake league. In all, there are ten teams located in California playing in the California League and 12 teams in Florida playing in the Florida State League. The eight teams playing in the Carolina League are spread across five states along the Atlantic Ocean from the Carolinas up to the Mason-Dixon line.

Perhaps most revealing in studying the regional nature of Class A Advanced-level baseball is the geographic dispersion of the teams in each of its three leagues. Specifically, we can define a simple measure of dispersion as the direct line distance, in miles, between the two outermost teams in each league. While not a perfect measure of the amount of travel teams within each of these leagues must endure throughout the season of play, it is at least a rough estimate of the size of the footprint that the league covers across a section of the US. That is, measuring dispersion as the distance between the outermost locations for each league gives us a metric that is likely correlated with the number of Major League Baseball teams that are close to the teams in the league at that particular level of play.

The three leagues at the Class A Advanced level of minor league baseball have the three smallest measures of dispersion of any of the leagues in the four levels of minor league baseball we are studying in this book. The Florida State League has the smallest footprint of all the leagues, with the distance between the two most extreme teams in the league—Daytona and Fort Myers—only 189 miles. With 371 miles between Stockton and Lake Elsinore, the California League has the next lowest measure of dispersion. Finally, the Carolina League, spread across five states on the Atlantic Coast, has a dispersion measure of 456 miles, which is the distance between Wilmington, Delaware, and Myrtle Beach, South Carolina.

Table 4.3 Distance in miles between outermost teams

Level	League	Outermost teams	Distance
Triple A	International	Indianapolis—Pawtucket	786
Triple A	Pacific Coast	New Orleans—Tacoma	2,082
Double A	Eastern	Akron—Portland	599
Double A	Southern	Jackson—Jacksonville	556
Double A	Texas	Corpus Christi—Springfield	693
Class A Advanced	California	Lake Elsinore—Stockton	371
Class A Advanced	Carolina	Myrtle Beach—Wilmington	456
Class A Advanced	Florida State	Daytona—Fort Myers	189
Class A	Midwest	Cedar Rapids—Lake County	527
Class A	South Atlantic	Lakewood—Rome	726

The dispersion measure for the other three levels of minor league baseball is included in Table 4.3, and shows the larger footprint each of the other leagues at the other levels of minor league baseball covers. The Triple A level has the largest footprint of all levels of the minor leagues, while the Double A and Class A levels are comparable in dispersion. Note, however, that having three leagues at the Double A level allows more opportunities for Major League Baseball teams to be located closer to a minor league affiliate than having just two leagues at the Class A level.

The relatively small footprint of the Class A Advanced leagues means that Major League Baseball teams in the Midwest and Northeast will not have many available minor league teams with which to enter into a possible affiliation. Attachment 58 to the Major League Rules only requires a stadium that can seat a minimum of 4,000 fans at the A level of baseball, so teams at the Class A Advanced level of minor league baseball tend to be located in much smaller population areas than either Triple A or Double A teams. Coupled with the small geographic dispersion of the teams in each league at the Class A Advanced level, it should come as no surprise that the Class A Advanced level required the most rounds of iterations compared to all the levels in order to assign each of the 30 Major League Baseball teams an affiliate.

Table 4.4 shows the Pareto efficient affiliation pairs for the Class A Advanced level. As with the Double A level, there are 13 Major League Baseball teams that are paired with the minor league team closest to them at the Class A Advanced level. These pairings are noted in the second column by the absence of any closer Class A Advanced teams in parentheses. Of particular note, there are only four affiliate pairs that are the same as those seen in Major League Baseball in 2014. These pairs are marked with an asterisk. The 13 Major League teams that are matched with their closest minor league team at this level represent almost half of the available teams, again suggesting that the algorithm used in the iterated allocation mechanism is fairly effective in assigning affiliate pairs to teams that are close to each other.

The aggregate distance for the Pareto efficient affiliate pairs is 17,126 miles. The mean and median distances between affiliate pairs are 571 and 489 miles, respectively. We can compare these distances to those from the current allocation of

Table 4.4 Class A Advanced Pareto efficient affiliate pairs

MLB team	PE affiliate (closer Class A Advanced teams)	Distance
Arizona	Inland Empire	303
Atlanta	Winston-Salem	289
Baltimore	Frederick*	45
Boston	Palm Beach (more than ten teams closer)	1,180
Chicago Cubs	Charlotte (more than ten teams closer)	1,081
Chicago White Sox	Lakeland (more than ten teams closer)	1,002
Cincinnati	Salem	269
Cleveland	Myrtle Beach (Frederick, Potomac, Salem, Lynchburg, Wilmington, Winston-Salem, Carolina)	559
Colorado	High Desert	773
Detroit	Brevard County (Frederick, Potomac, Salem, Lynchburg, Wilmington, Winston-Salem, Carolina, Daytona)	985
Houston	Dunedin	770
Kansas City	Fort Myers (more than ten teams closer)	1,132
Los Angeles Angels	Rancho Cucamonga	25
Los Angeles Dodgers	Lancaster (Rancho Cucamonga)	47
Miami	Jupiter*	80
Milwaukee	Bakersfield (more than ten teams closer)	1,731
Minnesota	Visalia (more than ten teams closer)	1,481
NY Mets	Carolina (Wilmington, Frederick, Potomac, Lynchburg, Salem)	418
NY Yankees	Daytona (Wilmington, Frederick, Potomac, Lynchburg, Salem, Carolina, Winston-Salem, Myrtle Beach)	898
Oakland	San Jose	33
Philadelphia	Wilmington	24
Pittsburgh	Lynchburg (Frederick, Potomac)	220
Saint Louis	Tampa (more than ten teams closer)	857
San Diego	Lake Elsinore*	64
San Francisco	Stockton (San Jose)	59
Seattle	Modesto (Stockton)	690
Tampa Bay	Clearwater	19
Texas	Bradenton (Dunedin, Clearwater, Tampa)	942
Toronto	St. Lucie (more than ten teams closer)	1,128
Washington	Potomac*	23

affiliation pairs. In 2014, the aggregate distance for all 30 Major League teams was 20,439 miles. Mean and median distances between affiliates were 681 and 892 miles, respectively. Thus, our iterated allocation mechanism cuts the mean distance between affiliate pairs by about one-sixth and cuts the median affiliate pair distance by nearly half. In Chapter 5, we will provide some alternative affiliate pairs that can cut the distances between affiliate pairs for some Major League teams from their 2014 pairings. We turn our attention now, finally, to the Class A level of baseball.

Class A Pareto Efficient Affiliate Pairs

The last level of minor league baseball we will examine is Class A. As with the Triple A level, there are only two leagues at the Class A level of baseball—the Midwest League and the South Atlantic League. But while the two Triple A-level leagues have coverage across the entire US, the two Class A-level leagues have virtually no footprint west of the Mississippi River or in the Northeastern part of the US. There are 13 Major League Baseball teams located west of the Mississippi River (two of these Major League teams are essentially located on the banks of the Mississippi River) and five Major League Baseball teams in the Northeast US. So over half of the teams at the Major League level are either west of the Mississippi River or in the Northeast part of the US. Conversely, the Cedar Rapids Kernels of the Midwest League is the only team at the Class A level west of the Mississippi River (three other teams in the Midwest League are located on the Mississippi River) and the South Atlantic League's Lakewood Blueclaws is the only team in Class A baseball located in the Northeast. Note that 9 of the 13 Major League teams west of the Mississippi River claim Cedar Rapids as the closest Class A-level team, but only one of those teams can be matched with the Kernels. Also, four of the five Major League teams in the Northeast claim Lakewood as their closest Class A-level team, but again, only one of them can be paired with the Blueclaws. It stands that this geographic phenomenon is primarily what leads to the large number of iterations required to match affiliate pairs in our allocation mechanism. More to the point, the picture that emerges very quickly at the Class A level is that the regional nature of the league structure significantly limits the number of Major League Baseball teams that can be matched with an affiliate that is relatively close in geographic proximity.

We can apply the same iterated allocation mechanism to Class A-level baseball in order to assign a set of Pareto efficient affiliate pairs to all 30 Major League Baseball teams. A total of 14 rounds of the iterative process were needed to assign an affiliate to each Major League Baseball team. It is not surprising that so many rounds of the iterative process were necessary given the lack of geographic dispersion of the Class A level. In this regard, Class A is much more similar to the Class A Advanced level, even though that level has three leagues instead of two.

Table 4.5 lists the affiliate pairs for each of the 30 Major League Baseball teams. Note that just 12 Major League Baseball teams are matched with the minor league team at the Class A level that is closest to them. This is the lowest number of Major League teams that are successfully matched with the closest minor league team at any level. But we can note that this number is close enough to our Pareto efficient affiliate pairs assigned in the other levels of minor league baseball to suggest a geographic dispersion among Major League Baseball teams that is able to overcome most difficulties in matching affiliates across a narrower dispersion of minor league teams. As in the previous tables describing the Pareto efficient pairs, these pairings are noted in the second column by the absence of any closer Class A teams in parentheses. Of particular note, there are nine affiliate pairs that are the same as those seen in

Table 4.5 Class A Pareto efficient affiliate pairs

MLB team	PE affiliate (closer Class A teams)	Distance
Arizona	Wisconsin (Burlington, Cedar Rapids, Quad Cities, Peoria, Clinton, Beloit, Kane County, Bowling Green)	1,470
Atlanta	Rome*	62
Baltimore	Hagerstown	63
Boston	Hickory (more than ten teams closer)	711
Chicago Cubs	Kane County*	36
Chicago White Sox	South Bend (Kane County)	72
Cincinnati	Dayton*	48
Cleveland	Lake County*	17
Colorado	Quad Cities (Cedar Rapids, Burlington)	760
Detroit	Lansing	79
Houston	Clinton (more than ten teams closer)	887
Kansas City	Burlington	218
Los Angeles Angels	Lexington (more than ten teams closer)	1,881
Los Angeles Dodgers	Asheville (more than ten teams closer)	2,016
Miami	Charleston (Savannah)	485
Milwaukee	Beloit	64
Minnesota	Cedar Rapids*	226
NY Mets	Lakewood	51
NY Yankees	Kannapolis (Lakewood, Delmarva, Hagerstown, Lake County, West Virginia)	516
Oakland	Greenville (more than ten teams closer)	2,209
Philadelphia	Greensboro (Lakewood, Delmarva, Hagerstown, Lake County, West Virginia)	365
Pittsburgh	West Virginia* (Lake County, Hagerstown)	170
Saint Louis	Peoria*	144
San Diego	Fort Wayne* (more than ten teams closer)	1,849
San Francisco	Augusta* (more than ten teams closer)	2,269
Seattle	West Michigan (Cedar Rapids, Burlington, Quad Cities, Clinton, Wisconsin, Beloit, Peoria, Kane County)	1,790
Tampa Bay	Savannah	312
Texas	Bowling Green (Burlington)	669
Toronto	Great Lakes (Lake County)	248
Washington	Delmarva (Hagerstown)	88

Major League Baseball in 2014. These pairs are marked with an asterisk. While we see the least success with getting larger numbers of Major League teams to be matched with the closest Class A-level minor league team in our Pareto efficient allocation mechanism, it is to be expected given the limited geographic coverage of the two leagues at this level.

The aggregate distance for the Pareto efficient allocation pairs presented in Table 4.5 is 19,775 miles. The mean and median distances are 659 and 280 miles, respectively.

The aggregate distance for the 2014 allocation of affiliate pairs among the 30 Major League teams is 21,597, and the mean and median distances are 720 and 613 miles, respectively. The mean distance between affiliate pairs drops by less than 10%, which suggests that there is some room for improving upon the current allocation of affiliate pairs. But noteworthy is that, more than any other level of minor league baseball, this Pareto efficient allocation mechanism was able to cut the median distance between affiliate pairs by more than half. This is a strong indication that centralized policy changes could lead to some very real benefits in the form of improving geographic proximity to the Class A affiliate for a non-negligible number of Major League Baseball teams. It is precisely this potential benefit that motivates our Chapter 5. We now turn our attention to proposing some affiliate switches, based on the 2014 affiliations, and policy changes that, if implemented, could lead to very real benefits for most Major League Baseball teams as they relate to player development, travel cost, and brand awareness. Note that a set of affiliation switches that were implemented in October 2014 are not considered in Chapter 5.

Chapter 5
Some Select Proposed Affiliation Switches

In the previous chapter, we developed an algorithm that allowed us to craft an allocation of affiliations between each of the 30 Major League Baseball teams and exactly one minor league baseball team at each classification level from Class A up to Triple A. The fundamental assumption directing how these affiliations were assigned centered on the distance between the Major League Baseball team and the minor league team with which it was being matched. Through an iterative process, we were able to match each Major League team with the closest minor league team available that was not already assigned to be an affiliate with another Major League team. It is important to note that the Pareto efficient allocation of affiliate pairs that results using this mechanism is not the only Pareto efficient allocation of affiliate pairs. However, given the focus on the benefits that can be realized upon establishing affiliations between Major League and minor league teams that are closest to each other, we can be confident that the allocations offered in Chap. 4 represent a type of baseline against which we can measure any suggested affiliation switches compared to the current allocation of affiliations.

In this chapter, we suggest some affiliation switches for each of the four full-season classification levels of minor league baseball. Each one of these switches would be expected to lead to benefits for the Major League teams involved. These benefits include, but are not limited to, an improved player development process, lower player and staff travel costs, and greater regional brand awareness.[1]

The nature of the current allocation of affiliations adds an important constraint to how these prescribed switches are determined. First, assume that the Pareto efficient affiliation schedules derived for each classification level in Chap. 4 are too drastic of a policy option to be implemented as a whole. The Pareto efficient schedules

[1] Note that these suggested affiliation switches are based on the 2014 allocation of affiliations. The affiliation switches that were announced in October 2014 are not used as a baseline comparison in this analysis. But they do suggest some of the important features that must be considered when seeking to form new affiliations between Major League Baseball teams and minor league baseball teams.

© Springer Science+Business Media New York 2015

T.A. Rhoads, *The Call Up to the Majors*, Sports Economics, Management and Policy 7, DOI 10.1007/978-1-4614-8924-5_5

developed in the previous chapter can thus be thought of as a "nuclear option" and there is at least one major reason why we do not want them implemented—many of the proposed affiliate pairs would result in longer distances from the Major League team to its affiliate when compared to the current setting. From a policy perspective, any kind of decision to scrap all of the existing affiliation assignments currently in place in favor of the schedules offered in Chap. 4 would require some Major League Baseball teams to be paired with a minor league team that is farther away than the current allocation. As the focus throughout this book centers on the benefits flowing from affiliate proximity, the nuclear option will not be considered an acceptable policy prescription. So even though decreasing aggregate distance between affiliates across all of Major League Baseball is a preferred outcome, all else equal, it should not be the result of increasing the distance to an affiliate for any other Major League Baseball team.

Instead of suggesting that Major League Baseball executives work towards implementing the Pareto efficient affiliate pairs from the previous chapter, we are going to suggest a set of affiliation switches to the current allocation of affiliate pairs that are more realistic. Specifically, we will work towards aligning affiliates in those situations that will result in closer affiliate proximity for one Major League Baseball team while not coming at the cost of greater distance to affiliate for another. This approach provides a realistic set of proposed affiliate switches that Major League Baseball executives could feasibly pursue. Making these switches would be expected to lead to some real benefits for each of the Major League Baseball teams involved.

There are a few assumptions we need to make that will place our suggested affiliate switches in the proper real-world setting. After all, for these suggestions to be taken seriously by Major League Baseball executives—and any other parties involved—and not simply be an academic exercise, there has to be some real-world context. Any affiliate switches that are proposed in this chapter must satisfy some simple requirements. These requirements center on three things: (1) the length of affiliation between the Major League Baseball team and its current minor league affiliate, (2) the distance between the affiliate pairs, and (3) the league and classification level of the affiliate minor league team.

Length of Affiliation

We'll first address the length of affiliation between a Major League and minor league baseball team. We will only consider those affiliation switches for which the current length of affiliation is no longer than 10 years. It goes without saying that for some Major League Baseball teams, the nature of the business relationship they have with their minor league affiliate is of paramount importance. Entering into a business contract, through the standard Player Development Contract, suggests a focus on certain joint business goals. We assume that the ownership of a Major League Baseball team desires their minor league baseball players to develop optimally towards being ready for play at the Major League level. This means that players will be moving up or down a level or two within the organization with little or no regard to the impact on the team that player is currently on or moving to. Additionally, the Major League ownership will want to move their players between levels as roster moves are required because of injury or poor performance on the Major League roster. Concurrently, the minor league baseball team ownership is focused on profitability. Filling the seats in the stadium with fans who pay for tickets and parking and stick around the ballpark long enough to buy concessions and souvenirs is an important component in the minor league team's profitability.

The goals of the owners of the Major League team and the minor league team that are paired as affiliates through a Player Development Contract are not necessarily mutually exclusive. But they are also sometimes easily misaligned. Winning minor league baseball teams at the Double A and Class A Advanced and Class A levels, for example, sees minimal increases in attendance.[2] And only the most elite of top prospects lead to minimally more attendance at the Triple A level only.[3] All of this suggests that minor league teams looking to increase profitability will likely find as much or more success by not focusing on the product on the field. However, the product on the field, and more specifically the link to the most valuable brand in professional baseball, is what largely brings fans to the minor league ballpark in the first place. In other words, the baseball product is necessary to bring the fans to the game, but the profitability of the minor league team is often the result of all the business decisions—marketing and promotions, for example—that are under the direction of the minor league ownership.

Typically, these Player Development Contracts are good for 2–4 years and can be renewed. Familiarity with the owner of the minor league team and the local community can make the affiliation and the accompanying joint business venture a relatively simple matter. Aligning with other teams in a particular league at the minor league can even be an important consideration for decision makers in the front office of a Major League Baseball team. Beyond these obvious benefits, there are intangibles that matter in a business partnership. Certain nonpecuniary benefits can, and do, exist for certain Major League Baseball teams that are independent of proximity to their minor league affiliate. Generally, these types of benefits can lead to repeated renewals of a Player Development Contract between a Major League and a minor league affiliate.

After taking all these benefits into consideration, we assume that longer affiliations likely suggest intangible benefits that are not easily quantified with lower travel costs, better quality player development, and more regional brand awareness. Because we

---

[2] In the work I did with Seth Gitter, we determined that winning teams at only the Double A and both Class A Advanced and Class A levels in full-season minor league baseball lead to higher attendance. But the number of additional fans in these settings amounted to much less than 100 fans per game—almost 50 fans at the Class A level and about 90 fans at the Double A level (Gitter and Rhoads 2010).

[3] Seth Gitter and I determined that only prospects rated in the top 5 by Baseball America in their listing of the Top 100 prospects increased attendance marginally at the Triple A level only (Gitter and Rhoads 2011).

have no way to easily measure those intangible benefits, we can only proxy for them and therefore provide a best estimate for identifying current affiliations that are beneficial to the Major League Baseball team, regardless of proximity to its affiliate. For those affiliations that are currently in at least the tenth year, it is assumed that certain nonpecuniary benefits are generated that suggest that continuing the affiliation is the preferred path for the Major League Baseball team, regardless of proximity. Of course, this assumption precludes us from considering affiliations that have been in effect for less than 10 years to be capable of generating significant benefits beyond those expected through adhering to the Player Development Contract. But the logistical difficulties of switching affiliations—one of which is finding another Major League Baseball team also willing to switch affiliations—suggest that affiliations lasting more than 10 years have effectively moved far enough along to have gone beyond a reasonable time for successfully switching out of an unwanted affiliation. Thus, we restrict our search for possible affiliation switches to those for which current affiliations are no greater than 10 years in duration.

Distance Between Affiliate Pairs

Next, we will only include those affiliate switches for which at least one of the Major League Baseball teams involved in the switch can cut the direct line distance to their affiliate by at least 5 % of the direct line distance to their current affiliate. Further, the other Major League Baseball teams involved in the affiliate switch may not increase the direct line distance to their new proposed affiliate by more than 1 % of the direct line distance to their current affiliate. And finally, in none of the switches may the aggregate distance between proposed affiliate minor league baseball teams and Major League Baseball teams be greater than it currently is. There are real costs to switching affiliations, so there need to be real benefits in the form of lower travel costs and for players and staff. These broad stipulations should help point out some reasonable affiliate switches that could be pursued.

Consider some simplified examples in the figures below of direct line distance between multiple locations to get a better sense of how to think about distance between affiliates. Assume two Major League teams—the A's and the B's—located in A and B, respectively. Also assume two minor league teams—the a's and the b's—located in a and b, respectively. All four locations—A, B, a, and b—are located along a straight line as illustrated below in Fig. 5.1. Let the distance from A to b and from B to a both be 250 miles and let the distance from b to B be 100 miles. The Pareto efficient allocation mechanism from the previous chapter would assign Bb and Aa as affiliate pairs. The distance between affiliate pair Aa is 600 miles and the distance between affiliate pair Bb is 100 miles, giving an aggregate distance between affiliates

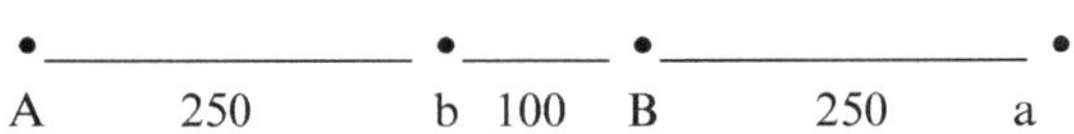

Fig. 5.1 Distance between affiliates

Fig. 5.2 Distance between affiliates

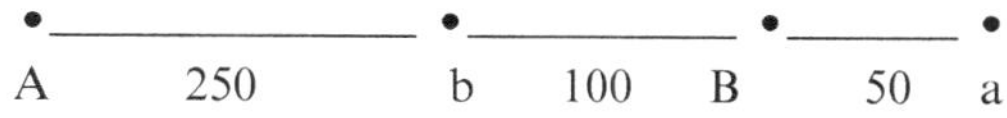

Fig. 5.3 Distance between affiliates

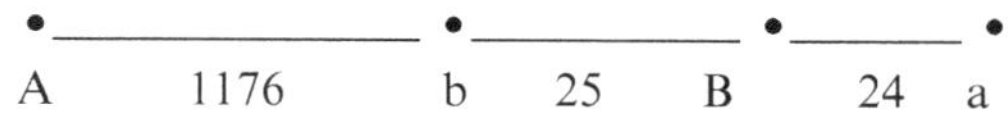

of 700 miles. This affiliate pair is considered Pareto efficient because switching affiliations to Ab and Ba would mean that Major League team B has a greater distance to affiliate than the original allocation. Note that the aggregate distance to affiliates for this new pairing—500 miles—is actually lower than for the original Pareto efficient pairing, and itself is a Pareto efficient allocation. Therefore, any recommended allocation scheme in Fig. 5.1 that is different from the current pairing would not be permitted because both of the possible affiliation allocations are Pareto efficient and there are no Pareto improvements to be realized.

Now consider another set of distances between locations of Major League and minor league baseball teams in Fig. 5.2. This time, the intent is to demonstrate a simple setting where a Pareto improving affiliation switch is possible. In this case, the direct line distance between B and a is 50 miles; in Fig. 5.1 this distance was 250 miles and the other distances were the same. Using our Pareto efficient allocation mechanism, minor league team a would be assigned as an affiliate to Major League team B, and minor League team b would be assigned as an affiliate to Major League team A.

But imagine, instead, if Major League team A and minor league team a were affiliates, leaving Major League team B and minor league team b to be affiliates. Clearly, there is a Pareto improving affiliation switch that can be made—match Major League team A with minor league team b and match Major League team B with minor league team a, just as in the Pareto efficient allocation described initially for Fig. 5.2. In fact, this affiliation switch leads to an improvement in proximity for both Major League teams. Major League team A is 150 miles closer to its affiliate when paired with minor league team b instead of minor league team a. And Major League team B is 50 miles closer to its affiliate when paired with minor league team a instead of minor league team b. It becomes obvious that as long as the distance between B and a is less than the distance between B and b, there will be a Pareto improving affiliation switch that is possible if the initial affiliate pairs are A with a and B with b.

Let's take a look at one more example of distances between affiliates in order to put a constraint on the minimum improvement in proximity required to propose an affiliation switch. Figure 5.3 below includes the same layout of Major League teams, A and B, and minor league teams, a and b, as we saw in the previous two examples. But the distances between locations A, b, B, and a are different now so that we can show that the magnitude of the decrease in distance matters when proposing an affiliation switch.

The Pareto efficient allocation mechanism introduced in the prior chapter gives us Major League team A paired with minor league team b and Major League team

B paired with minor league team a. The aggregate distance to affiliate for both Major League teams in this case is 1,200 miles—1,176 miles between A and b and 24 miles between B and a. But imagine if, instead, the alternative affiliate pairing of Aa and Bb is in place. Major League team A would be 1,225 miles from its affiliate minor league team a, and Major League team B would be 25 miles from its minor league affiliate b. Of course, a Pareto improvement is possible in this case by switching affiliations to Ab and Ba, which would now mean that Major League team A is 25 miles closer to its affiliate than previously and Major League team B is 1 mile closer to its affiliate than before. Thus, the aggregate distance to affiliate for both Major League teams is 1,250 miles. Clearly, the Pareto efficient allocation that matches each Major League team with its closest minor league team is preferred.

While both Major League teams have shorter distances to their affiliate using the Pareto efficient allocation mechanism, the distances between locations were arranged in Fig. 5.3 to suggest that maybe the costs of switching affiliations are not enough to offset the costs of making those changes. In other words, if the original affiliate pairs were Aa and Bb, the gains from switching affiliation pairs to Ab and Ba that would come in the form of lower travel costs for players and staff moving between the Major League team's location and the minor league team's location would likely not be greater than the costs of switching to a new affiliate. Those costs can include the legal costs and transaction costs that arise from ending an affiliation with one minor league team and entering into a new agreement through signing a Player Development Contract with a new minor league team. Administrative, bureaucratic, and even regulatory costs must be considered as well.

All of this suggests that there must be some minimal improvement in the distance between affiliate pairs for all of these costs to be covered by the lower travel costs, subsequent gains in player development, and regional brand value. For the purposes of this study, we will require a decrease of at least 5 % in the distance to affiliate for each of the Major League teams involved in an affiliation switch. Given the distances in Fig. 5.3, our requirement that distances between affiliate pairs decrease by at least 5 % is not met and therefore would not be suggested as a potential affiliate switch. Specifically, both Major League team A and B would see a decrease in the distance to affiliate of just 4 %. Cutting 49 miles for Major League team A from affiliate pair Aa, at 1,225 miles, to affiliate pair Ab, at 1,176 miles, is a 4 % decrease in distance. And cutting 1 mile for Major League team B—going from 25 miles to 24 miles as the switch is made from affiliate pair Bb to affiliate pair Ba—is a 4 % decrease in distance.

League of Affiliated Minor League Team

Already we have suggested that any proposed affiliation switch can occur only for Major League teams that have had affiliations lasting for no more than 10 years with their current minor league affiliate and that the decrease in distance between each affiliate pair must be at least 5 % of the current distance. The last requirement for

Table 5.1 Minor league changes and affiliation switches since 2007

	Triple A	Double A	Class A Advanced	Class A
2014	None	None	None	None
2013	2/2	None	None	2/7
2012	None	None	None	None
2011	0/2	None	2/5	0/2
2010	None	None	2/2	None
2009	0/3	0/3	2/2	2/4
2008	None	None	None	None
2007	2/5	2/4	4/6	2/4

any affiliate switch that we will propose in this chapter considers the league of play within which the minor league team plays. Each Major League Baseball team is currently affiliated with a minor league team that plays a full season of games in a league structure. For example, the Tampa Bay Rays Triple A affiliate, the Durham Bulls, play in the International League. While the Tampa Bay Rays are closer to the New Orleans Zephyrs by direct line distance than they are to the Durham Bulls (486 miles compared to 611 miles) and while the Pareto efficient allocation mechanism pairs the Rays with the Zephyrs, one major issue arises that prevents us from proposing an affiliation switch. The Zephyrs are in the Pacific Coast League. Because the Pacific Coast League and the International League are different—for one thing, the elevation where games are played in the Pacific Coast League leads to a different emphasis by pitchers throwing breaking balls instead of fastballs (Feinstein 2014)—switching from the International League to the Pacific Coast League has to be assumed an unrealistic proposed switch.[4] Therefore, we will not consider proposing any affiliate switch that would have Tampa Bay's Triple A affiliate playing in the Pacific Coast League.

It must be noted that many times the affiliation switches that have occurred since 2007 include a switch of the league in which the minor league team plays. Table 5.1 above provides detail on the number of affiliation switches that additionally included the Major League team switching the league of affiliation. In total, 22 of 51 affiliation switches that occurred since 2007 involved the Major League team changing the league to which their minor league affiliate belongs. For example, two of the five affiliate switches at the Triple A level in 2007 involved a league change for the Major League team's affiliate. So while it is not at all uncommon for Major League teams to switch the league of their affiliate, we will not suggest affiliation switches that lead to league changes in any of our proposals.

We can summarize the above discussion. We will not allow any league switches for any proposed affiliate switches, regardless of classification level and league. By keeping the primary focus on proximity in our analysis, not allowing league changes helps us try to keep constant the other factors that can influence why a

[4] Note that prior to the 2013 season the Toronto Blue Jays and New York Mets switched affiliates. The New York Mets' new affiliate became the Las Vegas 51's in the Pacific Coast League and the Toronto Blue Jays' new affiliate became the Buffalo Bisons in the International League. Thus, in switching Triple A affiliates, New York and Toronto also switched leagues at the Triple A level.

Major League Baseball team decides to enter into an affiliation agreement with a minor league team. The minor league in which an affiliate plays is thus assumed to be a function of the style of play the Major League team prefers, so any deviation from that league would address more than just the proximity issue that we have spent so much effort trying to get a handle on.

Now that we have set up the very strict parameters dictating the constraints on any affiliation switches, we can proceed to highlight those switches that fit within this construct. The proposed switches that follow represent some immediate real opportunities for the Major League Baseball teams involved. While the switches suggest that Major League Baseball's push towards regionalization is not yet complete, there are certainly some indications to suggest that regionalization is a high-order preference of Major League Baseball executives.

Finally, note that at the end of the following sections addressing each classification level, we also provide other possible affiliation switches that Major League Baseball executives should consider. In these other proposed switches, at least one of the strict constraints previously described could be lifted. As a result, more opportunities for regionalization to be achieved emerge. Of course, these other suggested affiliation switches will not be expected to get as much support among those Major League Baseball teams involved, but they do point out some remaining affiliation switches that could still provide benefits. We will start with highlighting the proposed switches at the Triple A level.

Proposed Triple A-Level Affiliation Switches

The Triple A level of minor league baseball has, by most measures, seen much progress in moving towards achieving a high degree of regionalization. As a result, there are only two Major League teams for which an affiliate switch is proposed that fits within the strict requirements laid out earlier in the chapter. However, eight more Major League teams could emerge from alternative affiliation switches with significant proximity benefits if the requirements guiding switches are relaxed. We will examine both sets of switches in turn.

Strictly Enforced Proposal

In 2014 the Los Angeles Dodgers were affiliated with the Albuquerque Isotopes and the Arizona Diamondbacks were affiliated with the Reno Aces. The Dodgers and Isotopes are 665 miles from each other and the Diamondbacks and Aces are 600 miles away. Each of these affiliations, in their current form, began in 2009.[5]

[5] The Aces moved to Reno from Tucson, Arizona, in 2009. In Tucson, the team had been named the Sidewinders and had been affiliated with the Diamondbacks since 1998. We treat the move to Reno as if the Diamondbacks began a new affiliation.

Table 5.2 Proposed Triple A-level affiliation switches

MLB team	Current affiliate (league)	Year affiliation began	Miles to current affiliate	Proposed affiliate (league)	Miles to proposed affiliate
Arizona Diamondbacks	Reno Aces (PCL)	2009	600	Albuquerque Isotopes (PCL)	330
Los Angeles Dodgers	Albuquerque Isotopes (PCL)	2009	665	Reno Aces (PCL)	387
New York Mets	Las Vegas 51s (PCL)	2013	2,234	Salt Lake Bees (PCL)	1976
Los Angeles Angels of Anaheim	Salt Lake Bees (PCL)	2001	578	Las Vegas 51s (PCL)	224
Pittsburgh Pirates	Indianapolis Indians (INTL)	2005	329	Rochester Red Wings (INTL)	223
Minnesota Twins	Rochester Red Wings (INTL)	2003	786	Indianapolis Indians (INTL)	512

A straight up switch of these affiliates between these two Major League Baseball teams would cut the direct line distance for each affiliate pair by nearly 300 miles. Table 5.2 above shows the current distance between affiliate pairs in addition to the distance between the proposed affiliate pairs. A proposed Dodgers and Aces affiliation would be 387 miles apart, which would be a decrease of 278 miles from the current setting—over 40 %—in distance to affiliate for the Dodgers. A proposed Diamondbacks and Isotopes affiliation would be 330 miles apart. This represents a drop in distance to affiliate for the Diamondbacks of 270 miles, which is 45 % of the current distance to affiliate for the Diamondbacks.

Cutting the distance to affiliate by close to half for the Dodgers and Diamondbacks would be a big deal since it makes travel by car a possibility that is not really feasible under the current affiliation scheme. Perhaps most attractive in offering this affiliate switch is that our Pareto efficient allocation mechanism introduced in the previous chapter pairs the Los Angeles Dodgers with the Reno Aces and the Arizona Diamondbacks with the Albuquerque Isotopes. Thus, an affiliation switch between the Dodgers and Diamondbacks would be seen as an additional push towards regionalization in Major League Baseball that is consistent with aligning Major League Baseball teams with their closest available minor league team at a given classification level. We next highlight the other affiliation switches at the Triple A level that may not be as attractive since they do not follow every one of the strict requirements laid out at the start of this exercise.

"Slim Chance" Proposals

The following suggested affiliation switches are presented in order to point to the robustness of our restrictive affiliation scenario. Again, we look at Table 5.2 to see the current and proposed affiliate switches. Each one of these proposed switches is understood to be less likely to be pursued by Major League Baseball or minor league baseball executives because at least one of the strict affiliation guiding constraints is ignored in crafting these switches. These proposals are presented to provide additional understanding of the difficulties baseball executives face in achieving a high level of regionalization by matching affiliate pairs in a way that allows Major League Baseball teams to affiliate with a minor league team that is close to them.

The first of these proposed affiliate switches, with what may be described as a slight chance of being implemented at best, involves the New York Mets and the Los Angeles Angels of Anaheim. The Mets have been affiliated with the Las Vegas 51's since 2013 and well over 2,000 miles separates this current affiliate pair. Switching the Mets affiliate is not expected to be problematic. On the other hand, the Angels have been affiliated with the Salt Lake Bees since 2001. Because of the Angels' nearly 15-year affiliation with the Bees, there may be significant nonpecuniary benefits accruing to the Angels through a business relationship that makes the relatively long distance to Salt Lake City feasible.

Because the Angels have continued to renew their Player Development Contract with the Bees for nearly 15 years, we must assume at least a satisfactory business relationship between the two teams. Being paired as affiliates since 2001 is notable because the median first year of affiliation for a Major League Baseball team with its Triple A affiliate is 2005. But there may be a good explanation for the rather long affiliation between the Angels and the Bees that does not rest on at least a satisfactory business relationship. More to the point, there may be a reason why the Angels have not signed a Player Development Contract with the Triple A affiliate in Las Vegas, which is the Triple A baseball team closest to them. This reason centers on the Major League teams that have alternatively been affiliated with the 51's throughout the years. The Los Angeles Dodgers were affiliated with the Las Vegas 51's from 2001 until 2008. From 2009 until 2012, the 51's were the Toronto Blue Jays Triple A affiliate, and now the Mets claim the 51's as their Triple A affiliate. A very important consideration in attempting to align affiliate switches is whether or not there are gains to be made for both Major League Baseball teams in the switching mix. From a proximity standpoint alone, switching affiliations with the Angels to gain the Salt Lake Bees as a Triple A affiliate would mean increasing distance between affiliates for the Dodgers, and it would be somewhat of a wash for switching with the Blue Jays or Mets.

Which brings us to why this proposed affiliate switch is listed as having only a "slim chance" of being implemented. The New York Mets would only decrease the distance to their Triple A affiliate by about 250 miles. Even though this diminished direct line distance would represent diminished time spent in travel, this is not even a 10 % decrease in distance and may not be enough of a cost savings to justify the additional benefits. For example, moving the Mets Triple A affiliate would likely do very little to aid in increasing the regional brand awareness for the Mets. Instead, the real advantage in this proposed switch belongs to the Angels. Going forward with this affiliation switch would mean matching the Angels with their closest minor league team at the Triple A level. A commitment by Major League Baseball to regionalize affiliates means that some Major League Baseball teams will be without a close minor league affiliate at every classification level. But this is not for lack of trying—trying to match affiliate pairs between Major League Baseball teams and a system of full-season professional baseball leagues at four levels of the minor leagues remains a function of the teams that currently exist. And the current geographic distribution of minor league baseball teams throughout the US simply leads to an outcome in which there will be some Major League Baseball teams with an affiliate that is not close. Unless there is a willingness to move baseball teams or reassign classification levels, this problem is likely to remain for the foreseeable future. We will focus a bit more on what these policy suggestions would mean for affiliated professional baseball towards the end of this chapter.

The second proposed affiliation switch that does not fit the strict guidelines and constraints laid out earlier involves the Pittsburgh Pirates and the Minnesota Twins. This affiliation switch does not appear likely to occur without some exogenous forces pushing towards this result along mostly because of the somewhat long affiliation between the Twins and their Triple A affiliate of over 10 years, the Rochester Red Wings. But a straight up swap of affiliates for the Pirates and Twins would lead to a decrease in direct line distance between affiliates for both Major League teams involved. Additionally, the Pirates would be aligned with the Triple A team that is assigned to them in the Pareto efficient allocation from the previous chapter. Overall, there may be enough benefits from making this affiliation switch and serious consideration should be given to making it happen.

The Pirates Triple A affiliate has been the Indianapolis Indians since 2005 and the Minnesota Twins Triple A affiliate has been the Rochester Red Wings since 2003. As shown in Table 5.2, 786 miles separates the Twins and the Red Wings, while there are only 512 miles between the Twins and the Indianapolis Indians. Switching the Twins Triple A affiliate from the Red Wings to the Indians would drop the direct line distance to affiliate by about one-third and would move the Twins Triple A affiliate out of the Northeast and relocate them into the Midwest. From a regional branding point of view, this move would seem to make sense. But the fact that the Twins and Red Wings have been joined by a Player Development Contract since 2003 suggests that a good business relationship exists between the two teams. Without being able to accurately quantify the costs of discarding this particular business relationship, it is difficult to attempt to engage in a simple benefit-cost analysis of the Twins switching affiliates from Rochester to Indianapolis. But if the decreased distance to affiliate and the increased regional branding lead to quantifiable benefits that exceed the cost of ending the business relationship between the Twins and Red Wings, this part of the affiliate switch makes sense.

The other half of this straight up switch is for the Pittsburgh Pirates to end their affiliation with the Indianapolis Indians and begin an affiliation with the Rochester Red Wings. Table 5.2 shows that switching the Pirates Triple A affiliate to Rochester would cut 106 miles, or about one-third, of the distance to their affiliate at this level. Note that the Pirates and Indians have been affiliated since 2005, which is beginning to suggest a decent business relationship between the two baseball teams. Finally, note that the Pirates and Red Wings are proposed as an affiliate pair in the Pareto efficient allocation mechanism developed in the previous chapter. This suggests that the closest available minor league team at the Triple A level is the Rochester Red Wings. Recall the discussion in Chap. 4 about how the algorithm for determining affiliate pairs is determined. There are closer baseball teams at the Triple A level to the Pirates than the Red Wings. In fact, there are three other Triple A-level baseball teams that are closer to Pittsburgh than the Rochester Red Wings. But the presence of so many other Major League Baseball teams in that part of the country leads the Pareto efficient allocation algorithm to match each of those Major League Baseball teams with the closest "available" minor league baseball team. Within the construct of the Pareto efficient allocation mechanism, being focused on available minor league baseball teams is an important distinction to highlight.

There are, of course, other potential affiliate switches we could consider here. For example, switching the affiliates among the Washington Nationals, Chicago White Sox, and Tampa Bay Rays would cut aggregate distance to the Triple A-level affiliates by about 150 miles, but this represents a decrease in direct line distance of only about 15 % for the teams involved. Further, Chicago and Tampa Bay each has an affiliation with their Triple A-level minor league team that goes back about 15 years. In fact, the only Triple A affiliate the Tampa Bay Rays has ever known has been the Durham Bulls. So while this example reminds us that there are still proximity gains to be made at the Triple A level, the costs that would need to be incurred to get these remaining affiliation switches to occur are likely too high to offset the benefits of the Major League teams being closer to their Triple A affiliate. We now move on to the Double A level, where we can again recommend some affiliation switches.

Proposed Double A-Level Affiliation Switches

Using the criteria that we developed at the start of this chapter, we can propose just one switch at the Double A level. But we do offer one other affiliate switch to highlight what appears to be the importance of the business relationship between the Major League team and its minor league affiliate. The affiliate switches we will recommend here are unique in that aggregate distance to Double A affiliates across all of Major League Baseball can actually drop lower than that seen in the Pareto efficient allocation mechanism developed in the previous chapter. The reason we can achieve such gains in proximity rests solely in the current allocation of affiliates—the current distribution of affiliates at the Double A level includes some Major League teams that are paired up with an affiliate that is much closer than the Pareto efficient allocation mechanism would recommend. Thus, the starting point for determining allocation switches is much closer to the allocation found in the Pareto efficient allocation mechanism. If implemented, these two straight up switches would allow four Major League Baseball teams to be closer to a Double A affiliate by an average of 120 miles.

We begin by proposing a straight up affiliation switch between the Tampa Bay Rays and Cincinnati Reds Double A-level affiliates. Currently the Rays and Reds

Table 5.3 Proposed Double A-level affiliation switches

MLB Team	Current affiliate (league)	Year affiliation began	Miles to current affiliate	Proposed affiliate (league)	Miles to proposed affiliate
Cincinnati Reds	Pensacola Blue Wahoos (SOU)	2012	620	Montgomery Biscuits (SOU)	475
Tampa Bay Rays	Montgomery Biscuits (SOU)	2004	389	Pensacola Blue Wahoos (SOU)	332
New York Mets	Binghamton Mets (EAS)	1992	143	New Britain Rock Cats (EAS)	85
Minnesota Twins	New Britain Rock Cats (EAS)	1995	1,053	Binghamton Mets (EAS)	891

Double A affiliates are the Montgomery Biscuits and the Pensacola Blue Wahoos. The Biscuits have been the Double A affiliate of the Rays since 2004 and the Blue Wahoos have been the Reds' affiliate since 2012. Note that the Blue Wahoos were a new team in the Southern League in 2012, having replaced the Carolina Mudcats. Before their affiliation with the Blue Wahoos, the Reds were affiliated with the Mudcats since 2009. Table 5.3 shows the current and proposed affiliation switches for Double A. In switching from the Blue Wahoos to the Biscuits, the Reds would cut the distance to the Double A affiliate by 145 miles, which is nearly 25 % closer than its current distance of 620 miles to Pensacola, Florida. At 332 miles away instead of 389 miles away, the Rays' proposed affiliate would be almost 15 % closer. Although the Rays' proposed affiliate is not even 60 miles closer, the affiliate switch would match two Florida teams as affiliates. Further, the Blue Wahoos, if they were to become the Rays Double A affiliate, would place the Rays' affiliate in their own home television market. This could be a significant advantage in building the Rays' regional brand value across the state of Florida. Note that currently the Biscuits, located in Montgomery, Alabama, are in the Atlanta Braves home television market, so switching these affiliates would likely benefit the Rays' organization in multiple ways.

The other proposed Double A affiliate switch involves the New York Mets and the Minnesota Twins. The likelihood of this switch being attractive, however, to both Major League teams is considerably lower than the previous switch we examined because of the length of affiliation of these teams. This proposed switch does not, therefore, satisfy all the conditions laid out at the start of the chapter meant to guide affiliate switches. Both the Mets and the Twins and their Double A affiliates have been paired together for about 20 years. In fact, only three Major League teams—the Phillies, White Sox, and Indians—have longer affiliations at the Double A level than the Mets. And just one other team—the Orioles—can be added to this list of teams with a longer Double A affiliation than the Twins.

Resistance to a proposed affiliation switch between the Mets and Twins Double A teams would therefore be expected on the likely strength of the business relationship between the involved teams. That is, the length of affiliation between the

New York Mets and the Binghamton Mets and between the Minnesota Twins and the New Britain Rock Cats suggests that the benefits of the business relationship are greater than any travel costs associated with the distance to affiliate. While the Mets have the potential to cut more than a third of the distance to affiliate and expand their regional brand awareness into Connecticut, the Twins would really only benefit by cutting the distance to affiliate by about 15 %. Again, there are potentially real gains to be made by cutting the distance to affiliate for both the Mets and the Twins. But these gains would only come at the cost of ending a rather long affiliation for both Major League teams. This is unlikely, but it is at least worth proposing this switch in order to highlight the importance of the business relationship between an affiliate pair. Additionally, this proposed switch suggests an avenue for future research that could try to estimate the value of the business relationships between Major League Baseball teams and their minor league affiliates.

Finally, it must be noted that another potential affiliate switch appears attractive were it not for the ownership situation of the teams involved. The Mississippi Braves are the Double A affiliate of the Atlanta Braves and the Chattanooga Lookouts are the Double A affiliate of the Los Angeles Dodgers. Switching these affiliates could lead to almost 500 aggregate miles in closer proximity benefits for these affiliate pairs. However, the Mississippi Braves are operated by the Atlanta National League Baseball Club. One of the features typically found in the affiliation profile has been a separation between the product on the field—that is the baseball players and coaches—and how the baseball package is presented as entertainment by the ownership of the minor league team. Art Solomon, author of Making it in the Minors and owner of the Eastern League's New Hampshire Fisher Cats, writes, "It was clear to me from the first day of Fisher Cats ownership that the staff and I could not control what happened on the field because our Major League parent club is in charge of which players are on the team. We have had to focus on making the experience of coming to the ballpark as interesting and entertaining as possible." The Mississippi Braves is one of the few minor league teams owned and operated by the Major League affiliate, which means that the baseball on the field and the marketing of that baseball as entertainment are handled by the same organization. It is assumed that the Atlanta Braves organization would not prefer to market the entertainment value of the baseball on the field for their Double A-level baseball team when the players on that team were from another Major League Baseball team. As such, it would only appear that a switch of affiliates between the Braves and the Dodgers would only occur if both minor league ownership groups would also be willing to switch the location of their minor league teams, that is, for the Braves to move their minor league team to Chattanooga, Tennessee, and for the Lookouts to move their club to Pearl, Mississippi. This is highly doubtful, but points to the very unique relationship that Major League Baseball and minor league baseball teams have—a relationship that is largely a function of the high value to the minor league team of being associated with the most valuable brand in professional baseball. We now turn our attention to Class A Advanced-level baseball and the affiliation switches that are possible there.

Proposed Class A Advanced-Level Affiliation Switches

The Class A Advanced level of minor league baseball has three leagues—the California, Carolina, and Florida State Leagues. As we suggested in the prior chapter on affiliations, nearly all of the Major League teams with an affiliate in the Florida State League have their spring training located in the same facility as their minor league team. Only the Chicago Cubs, whose affiliate at the Class A Advanced level in 2014 was the Daytona Cubs in the Florida State League, have their spring training in Arizona's Cactus League. Milwaukee's Florida State League affiliate, the Brevard County Manatees, plays home games at Space Coast Stadium in Viera, Florida. While the Brewers are in Arizona's Cactus League for spring training, the Washington Nationals use the facilities at Space Coast Stadium for spring training. It is important to note the relationships between these teams in the Florida State League and Major League Baseball. While most of the affiliate pairs are much farther away than they otherwise could be given the available teams in the Carolina League, for example, there is a benefit to the Major League team in developing their minor league players at the Class A Advanced level at Major League-quality facilities in the Florida State League. As such, we will not recommend any affiliate switches for Major League teams currently affiliated with a team in the Florida State League.

Two recommended affiliate switches arise from our proposal guidelines. In total, these two straight up affiliate switches could cut almost 900 miles in aggregate distance between the affiliate pairs. This suggests that four Major League Baseball teams could be located an average of over 200 miles closer to their Class A Advanced-level affiliate if these proposed switches were made.

The first affiliate switch we propose involves the Colorado Rockies and the Seattle Mariners. Both teams have their Class A Advanced affiliate in the California League. Since 2007, the Mariners affiliate has been the High Desert Mavericks, located in Adelanto, California. The Rockies began their affiliation with the Modesto Nuts in 2005. A straight up affiliation switch between these two Major League teams would yield lower distances between the affiliate pairs and nothing else of note. The proposed new affiliates would not be any closer to other minor league teams in the proposed new Major League team's organization. As can be seen in Table 5.4 below, the Rockies would be more than 100 miles closer to a proposed new affiliate in Adelanto, a location that would put the Rockies' proposed Class A Advanced affiliate more than 10 % closer to Denver, Colorado, than the current affiliate. On the other side of this proposed affiliate swap, the Mariners would be more than 25 % closer—236 miles—to their new proposed affiliate.

The other straight up affiliate switch to recommend is between the Boston Red Sox and the Kansas City Royals. The Red Sox began their affiliation with the Class A Advanced Salem Red Sox in the Carolina League in 2009. The Royals and the Carolina League's Wilmington Blue Rocks began their affiliation in 2007. The Salem Red Sox are located in Salem, Virginia, and the Wilmington Blue Rocks are based in Wilmington, Delaware. As seen in Table 5.4, Boston could cut the distance

Table 5.4 Proposed Class A Advanced-level affiliation switches

MLB team	Current affiliate (league)	Year affiliation began	Miles to current affiliate	Proposed affiliate (league)	Miles to proposed affiliate
Colorado Rockies	Modesto Nuts (CAL)	2005	875	High Desert Mavericks (CAL)	773
Seattle Mariners	High Desert Mavericks (CAL)	2007	926	Modesto Nuts (CAL)	690
Boston Red Sox	Salem Red Sox (CAR)	2009	592	Wilmington Blue Rocks (CAR)	293
Kansas City Royals	Wilmington Blue Rocks (CAR)	2007	1,013	Salem Red Sox (CAR)	790

to their affiliate by more than half if this proposed switch was made; Kansas City could cut nearly one-quarter of the distance to affiliate.

To be sure, these are significant proximity advantages to be realized. But there may be one important reason why the Boston Red Sox would not want to enter into this proposed affiliate switch. Or, to put it another way, there may be an important reason why Boston is currently affiliated as they are with Salem. As Boston's Class A Advanced affiliate in Salem, the Red Sox Carolina League affiliate is currently about 200 miles away from Greenville, South Carolina. Boston's Class A affiliate is the Greenville Drive and some beneficial proximity considerations are to be assumed regarding the organizational relationship between the Salem Red Sox and the Greenville Drive. For example, as players move between these two levels of the Red Sox organization, travel costs will be lower and the players may likely be moved in an optimal fashion as it relates to player development. Further, travel costs for Red Sox front-office staff checking on progress at these two teams could be lower than with a proposed affiliation switch because Greenville is closer to Salem than it is to Wilmington.

Finally, we examine more closely how the proposed affiliation switch would affect the Kansas City Royals. And we can use the same line of argument as with the Boston Red Sox to suggest that the Royals may actually prefer this proposed affiliation. While the decreased distance from Kansas City to the proposed affiliate in Salem, Virginia, would be expected to lead to lower travel costs for players and staff, these savings are not as dramatic as the savings the Red Sox would experience. But there is a potentially more sizable benefit in this proposed affiliation switch as the proposed Royals Class A Advanced affiliate in Salem would now be about half the distance to the Class A affiliate in Lexington, Kentucky. Lower travel costs for players and staff as they move between these two levels of the Royals organization would make optimal player development more likely. The two straight up affiliation switches proposed in this section have highlighted the structural dynamics of the Major League team's organization. We turn our attention now to the lowest level of full-season minor league baseball to recommend some final straight up affiliation switches.

Proposed Class A-Level Affiliation Switches

In making recommendations for affiliation switches for Class A-level minor league baseball, we want to keep in mind some of the things we have learned to this point about current affiliations across all of Major League Baseball. Clearly, the benefits of closer proximity to the minor league affiliate are not without cost for the Major League team. For instance, the length of affiliation is often a function of the quality of the business relationship between the Major League team and its minor league affiliate. Any recommendation to break up a solid business relationship must have some important caveats attached. In fact, these caveats are the guidelines we have used for recommending affiliation switches. How much closer will the proposed affiliate be? Is the new affiliate in the same minor league as the current affiliate at that classification level? Will the proposed affiliate be in closer proximity to other minor league teams in the same organization?

Two straight up affiliation switches are recommended at the Class A level of minor league baseball. All four of the minor league teams involved in these proposed switches are members of the South Atlantic League. The first switch we present here offers only minor direct proximity advantages to be realized for both Major League teams involved. The real advantage in proposing this affiliate switch comes in locating the proposed Class A-level minor league team within each organization closer to its Class A Advanced-level team. The Boston Red Sox are currently affiliated with the Greenville Drive. As shown in Table 5.5, Boston and Greenville, South Carolina, are 799 miles apart. A proposed affiliation with the Crawdads in Hickory, North Carolina—the current Class A affiliate of the Texas Rangers—would move Boston almost 90 miles closer to a Class A-level minor league affiliate.

This recommended affiliation switch represents a distance savings of over 10 % between the Red Sox and the proposed Class A-level affiliate in Hickory. By itself, this may not be enough of a cost savings to warrant making the affiliation switch. However, matching the Red Sox with the Hickory Crawdads would place Boston's proposed Class A-level affiliate just 124 miles away from its current Class A Advanced-level affiliate in Salem, Virginia. Cutting nearly 100 miles of the current

Table 5.5 Proposed Class A-level affiliation switches

MLB team	Current affiliate (league)	Year affiliation began	Miles to current affiliate	Proposed affiliate (league)	Miles to proposed affiliate
Boston Red Sox	Greenville Drive (SAL)	2005	799	Hickory Crawdads (SAL)	711
Texas Rangers	Hickory Crawdads (SAL)	2009	922	Greenville Drive (SAL)	854
Miami Marlins	Greensboro Grasshoppers (SAL)	2003	711	Savannah Sand Gnats (SAL)	436
New York Mets	Savannah Sand Gnats (SAL)	2007	722	Greensboro Grasshoppers (SAL)	455

distance between these two teams within the organization—down from the current 211 miles from Greenville to Salem—can lead to lower travel costs for players and staff while likely providing more opportunities for optimal player assignments.

As the other Major League team in this suggested straight up switch, the Texas Rangers are currently affiliated with the Hickory Crawdads. Table 5.5 shows that a proposed switch from Hickory to Greenville would put the Rangers 68 miles closer to their Class A affiliate. This switch represents less than 10 % of the distance to the current affiliate. Further, Greenville is about 15 miles further from the Pelicans, the Rangers' Class A Advanced affiliate in Myrtle Beach in 2014. So there are no gains in proximity to be made across the Class A levels within the Rangers' organization. But the proposed move would put both Class A-level minor league affiliates for the Rangers in South Carolina, which could provide some benefits by itself. For example, regional brand awareness could become more defined within the state of South Carolina if the Texas Rangers were the parent Major League team for two of the three minor league teams in the entire state of South Carolina.[6]

The last proposed affiliate switch we suggest in this chapter is between the Miami Marlins and the New York Mets. The Class A-level affiliate for the Marlins since 2003 has been the Greensboro Grasshoppers, so this recommended switch does not strictly follow the criteria guiding our proposals—the Marlins have been affiliated with the Grasshoppers for more than 10 years. But the savings in travel distance to affiliate may be enough to offset any kind of lost benefits that would result from ending a potentially solid business relationship. In Table 5.5, we see that switching Miami's affiliate to the Sand Gnats in Savannah, Georgia, places the proposed Class A-level affiliate 275 miles closer than previously. This is a nearly 40 % cut in travel distance between Miami and its minor league affiliate, which is enough to suggest that this move could lead to travel cost savings. On the other side of the proposed switch, the New York Mets have been affiliated with the Savannah Sand Gnats since 2007. The Mets could move 267 miles closer to their affiliate at this level with a proposed affiliation with the Grasshoppers in Greensboro, North Carolina. So this proposed move would put the Mets more than 35 % closer in direct line distance to their Class A-level affiliate, which suggests opportunities for lower travel costs associated with player development.

The proposed affiliate switches highlighted in this chapter point to the unique relationship between Major League Baseball and minor league baseball. But more important perhaps, the proposed switches point to the need for additional research into the impact that Major League Baseball's antitrust exemption has on a Major League Baseball team's business relationship and player development decisions with each of their minor league affiliate teams. Player development costs are real, and cutting the distance between a Major League team and its minor league affiliate can cut those costs. Further, cutting the distance to other teams in the organization can provide optimal player development opportunities as players can move up and down with little resistance caused by geographic dispersion. The affiliate switches

[6]The Charleston Riverdogs in Charleston, South Carolina, are the Class A-level affiliate of the New York Yankees.

proposed in this chapter show that there are still potential benefits available for some Major League Baseball teams by decreasing the distance to their affiliate. The final chapter provides some suggestions for where the future of proximity-based economic analysis of professional affiliated baseball can and should go. We turn our attention there now.

Chapter 6
What Does This All Mean and Where Do We Go From Here?

Before reading through the results of the research in this book, the casual observer of the professional baseball industry would have already suspected that proximity matters at all levels of professional baseball. After all, drawing fans to the ballpark is a critical piece of a revenue-maximizing strategy for any professional sports team. With an antitrust exemption granted to them by the US Supreme Court nearly 100 years ago, Major League Baseball teams have considerable power in deciding where affiliated professional baseball teams can be located. In fact, very precise Major League Rules clearly mandate a minimum distance between home territories and home stadiums for all teams at all levels of affiliated baseball. By strategically locating affiliated professional baseball teams so that they can avoid competing for baseball fans to attend games, owners of affiliated baseball teams can increase ticket prices without the risk of losing too many fans to a competing professional baseball team. In the end, this can provide a higher stream of revenues for all affiliated professional baseball teams.

But there is some tension in this strategy of keeping a minimum distance between affiliated professional baseball teams. Because affiliated minor league baseball teams serve as the primary player development grounds for Major League Baseball teams, there is, in some sense, a need for each Major League Baseball team to be relatively close in geographic proximity to each of their affiliated minor league teams. This allows for optimal player development strategies to be driven by something other than the costs of moving players between levels within the minor league system and, ultimately, up to the Major League level. Of course, locating a minor league team too close to any Major League Baseball team is likely to result in decreased ticket sales for the minor league team because they are substitutes (Gitter and Rhoads 2010). And herein lies the trade-off that I've tried to highlight in this book. Proximity matters in professional baseball at the minor league level and at the Major League level. The extent to which Major League Baseball teams seek out affiliations with the closest available minor league teams offers insight into how important proximity for player development purposes really is. Further, the effect of proximity on attendance at the minor league level provides a sense of how important

© Springer Science+Business Media New York 2015
T.A. Rhoads, *The Call Up to the Majors*, Sports Economics, Management and Policy 7, DOI 10.1007/978-1-4614-8924-5_6

proximity is for limiting the amount of competing products. In both cases, the research in this book has offered a glimpse into this most unique and fascinating setting in professional sports.

There are some questions that naturally arise after spending so much time studying the economics of minor league baseball with a focus on the locational affiliation choices of Major League Baseball teams. It is not inconsequential that minor league baseball provides a superior natural setting in which to study how proximity matters in professional baseball. With the success of minor league baseball teams being so dependent on drawing fans to attend the games, we can observe rather precisely how certain aspects of locational proximity can impact attendance. Previous research already told us that winning matters some and new stadiums matter even more in attracting fans to minor league baseball games (Gitter and Rhoads 2010, 2014). What exactly do the results from this proximity-based approach to studying the economics of minor league baseball provide for us that we have not already learned? What lessons and analytical techniques can be applied within and beyond the arena of professional baseball?

The results from the research in this book suggest that while Major League Baseball teams seem to be moving generally towards affiliating with minor league teams that are closer in proximity, there is still considerable room for improvement. And, in fact, it appears that much of the remaining gains to be made in affiliating with the closest available minor league baseball team would require some central organizing structure to coordinate the necessary moves. Already, the Commissioner's Office in Major League Baseball is tasked with matching Major League Baseball teams with minor league baseball teams that are not yet affiliated and still need to enter into an affiliation through a Player Development Contract. Extending this capacity beyond just those occasions when a match is unable to be negotiated would perhaps provide for a better opportunity to achieve the optimal level of player development across all of Major League Baseball. Of course, the reality of the business side of professional baseball suggests that sometimes the closest available minor league team is not always the best match of front-office staff between both teams. And certain Major League Baseball teams may strategically affiliate with minor league teams in order to prevent other Major League Baseball teams from capturing the benefits afforded by affiliation with a close-proximity minor league team.

In order to proceed more directly with a central organizing body directing affiliations between Major League Baseball teams and minor league teams, a deeper understanding of how proximity impacts player development, regional brand awareness, and minor league game day attendance is needed. For example, we already know from previous research that fans can treat Major League Baseball games and minor league baseball games as close substitutes. One strategy to minimize the potentially negative impact on minor league (and to some degree Major League) attendance for those teams that are in close proximity to another affiliated professional baseball team is to have a central organizing body, like the Commissioner's Office, build the schedules of games at all levels of affiliated baseball in a way that minimizes the number of times that teams within close proximity of each other play on the same day. At the margin, this would be expected to provide a slight boost in attendance at all levels of affiliate professional baseball. Moreover, this simple example emphasizes how a unified approach to drawing fans to the ballpark for all levels of affiliated professional baseball requires central planning with a goal of maximizing aggregate attendance. The remainder of this chapter provides some suggestions to direct future research in this field of study.

Future Research Opportunities

There are some directions that proximity-based analysis will likely proceed over the next 5–10 years within the professional baseball arena. Future research can be expected to examine more deeply the gains in player development that come from closer proximity to the parent Major League Baseball team. Future research will at least be partly motivated by recognizing the limits to the current research and the techniques behind that research. To begin, there are some obvious limits to simply computing straight line distance between baseball stadiums using zip code data. For example, the Bluefield (West Virginia) Blue Jays and Burlington (North Carolina) Royals are separated by a straight line distance of 126 miles. While this distance compares well to the straight line distance between the San Antonio (Texas) Missions and Corpus Christi (Texas) Hooks, the terrain between each set of cities is quite different, and a drive between the two Appalachian League teams noted above would be expected to take potentially 50 % more time (nearly 3 h) than the drive between the two Texas League teams (about 2 h). Recognizing the limits to the current research thus allows us to see the direction that future research can go. We can point out some of those possibilities here.

Perhaps the most obvious direction to go in this field is to begin using GIS—geographic information system—data techniques in order to match the closest available minor league teams with each Major League Baseball team. GIS tools could provide more precision in studying the impact of proximity on attendance at minor league baseball games. GIS could also be used to make certain policy prescriptions that could lead to better player development opportunities for Major League Baseball teams. Many facets of the proximity story that have not been touched on yet could be handled quite easily using currently available GIS analytics. Using maps to interpret, analyze, predict, and prescribe policy within the professional baseball arena could lead to a more precise assessment of how the current affiliations stand compared to the optimal allocation of affiliations.

Another natural direction to take proximity-based economic research is to assess the impact of independent league baseball on affiliated minor league baseball and speculate on various permutations of the current system that is already in place. The results introduced earlier in Chap. 2 suggest that independent league baseball teams that are in closer proximity to each other experience an increase in attendance. Perhaps more fans have an opportunity to attend away games when the teams are located closer to each other. If this is indeed the case, this result suggests that the current Major League Rules mandating all affiliated baseball teams at the Major

League level and the minor league level to not be close to each other is an excessive restriction that does not need to be in place.

Further, there may be some consideration given to allowing a type of promotion and relegation system in minor league baseball that allows teams to move in and out of independent baseball and into and out of affiliated minor league baseball. Many of the independent league baseball teams are generally in relatively close proximity to major population areas. More to the point, these independent league baseball teams are very often relatively close to affiliated minor league baseball teams and to Major League Baseball teams and could potentially step up to be a part of affiliated professional baseball. A system of promotion and relegation would be a completely novel concept for baseball fans in the US to have to become familiar with, but the system seems to have worked well in other parts of the world with professional soccer leagues. Moreover, promotion and relegation can lead to exciting opportunities for fans. There could be a very large upside to the independent league teams with an opportunity to become an affiliated professional baseball team. It is likely that this system would be considered by many in the baseball industry to be too much of a shock to the current structure. Independent baseball leagues are really the only professional baseball leagues that are in expansion mode right now. The Atlantic League is in the process of expanding from 8 teams to 12 teams. Even so, decision makers within affiliated professional baseball must consider the implications of ignoring completely the burgeoning niche within professional baseball that independent league baseball is quickly filling.

I would like to think of this book as simply the first significant step in taking a proximity-based look at the economics of minor league baseball. There is still much to understand about how the industry is already structured to maximize player development opportunities and generate increasing attendance. The lessons learned here will allow those involved with the minor league baseball industry to remain focused on what matters most to the success of minor league baseball—maintaining and enhancing minor league baseball's entertainment value to baseball fans across the US—while not ignoring the proper place of minor league baseball in developing the next cohort of stars that will play in Major League Baseball.

References

Anthony, T., Kahn, T., Madison, B., Paul, R. J., & Weinbach, A. (2014). Similarities in fan preferences for minor-league baseball across the American Southeast. *Journal of Economics and Finance, 38*(1), 150–163.

Atlantic League Announces 2015 Schedule. (2014). Retrieved on October 30, 2014, from http://atlanticleague.com/news-league/news-league.aspx?ID=827.

J. Leventhal (Ed.) (2006–2014). Baseball America Directory.

Bradbury, J. C. (2007). *The baseball economist: The real game exposed*. New York, NY: Dutton.

Bradbury, J. C. (2011). *Hot stove economics: Understanding baseball's second season*. New York, NY: Springer Science+Business Media.

Brickley, J. A., & Dark, F. H. (1987). The choice of organizational form: The case of franchising. *Journal of Financial Economics, 18*(2), 401–420.

Brown, M. (2014). Through July, MLB telecasts on regional sports networks dominate prime time TV. Retrieved August 11, 2014, from http://www.forbes.com/sites/maurybrown/2014/08/05/mlb-telecasts-on-regional-sports-networks-dominate-prime-time-television/.

Burger, J. D., & Walters, S. K. (2009). Uncertain prospects: Rates of return in the baseball draft. *Journal of Sports Economics, 10*(5), 485–501.

Calandro, T. (2013). The cardinal way: Built to last. Retrieved November 7, 2013, from http://www.huffingtonpost.com/tony-calandro/the-cardinal-way-built-to_b_4164652.html.

Crasnick, J. (2013). Combining talent with intelligence. Retrieved November 7, 2013, from http://espn.go.com/mlb/story/_/id/9228234/manny-machado-true-disciple-oriole-way.

Davis, M. (2006). Called up to the big leagues: An examination of the factors affecting the location of minor league baseball teams. *International Journal of Sport Finance, 1*(4), 253–264.

Davis, M. (2007). Income and the locations of AAA minor league baseball teams. *Atlantic Economic Journal, 35*(3), 371–372.

Feinstein, J. (2014). *Where nobody knows your name: Life in the minor league of baseball*. New York, NY: Doubleday.

Freehling, B. (2013). Hagerstown Suns apply to relocate to Fredericksburg. Retrieved from November 7, 2013, from http://www.fredericksburg.com/business/business_insider/hagerstown-suns-apply-to-relocate-to-fredericksburg/article_5c883a16-0969-51e4-b1cc-aba7664a6539.html.

Ghiroli, B. (2014). Hunter to return Sunday, after rehab assignment. Retrieved June 18, 2014, from http://www.orioles.mlb.com/news/article/78414130/hunter-to-return-sunday-after-rehab-assignment.

Gifis, L. S., & Sommers, P. M. (2006). Promotions and attendance in minor league baseball. *Atlantic Economic Journal, 34*(4), 513–514.

© Springer Science+Business Media New York 2015

T.A. Rhoads, *The Call Up to the Majors*, Sports Economics, Management and Policy 7, DOI 10.1007/978-1-4614-8924-5

Gitter, S. R., & Rhoads, T. A. (2010). Determinants of minor league baseball attendance. *Journal of Sports Economics, 11*(6), 614–628.

Gitter, S. R., & Rhoads, T. A. (2011). Top prospects and minor league baseball attendance. *Journal of Sports Economics, 12*(3), 341–351.

Gitter, S. R., & Rhoads, T. A. (2014). Stadium construction and minor league baseball attendance. *Contemporary Economic Policy, 32*(1), 144–154.

http://atlanticleague.com/about.html. Accessed 23 October 2014.

Kalnins, A., & Lafontaine, F. (2013). Too far away? The effect of distance to headquarters on business establishment performance. *American Economic Journal: Microeconomics, 5*(3), 157–179.

Kroc, R. (1977). *Grinding it out: The making of McDonald's*. Chicago, IL: Contemporary Books, Inc.

Lafontaine, F. (1992). Agency theory and franchising: Some empirical results. *RAND Journal of Economics, 23*(2), 263–283.

Lewis, M. (2003). *Moneyball*. New York, NY: W.W. Norton & Company.

Longley, N., & Wong, G. (2011). The speed of human capital formation in the baseball industry: The information value of minor-league performance in predicting major-league performance. *Managerial and Decision Economics, 32*(3), 193–204.

MiLB.com frequently asked questions. (2014). Retrieved March 3, 2014, from http://www.milb.com/milb/info/faq.jsp?mc=business.

Nationals extend working agreements with four minor-league affiliates, Press Release|March 16, 2012. (2012). Retrieved November 7, 2013, from http://www.nationals.mlb.com/news/article/27335510/nationals-extend-working-agreements--with-four-minor-league-affiliates.

O'Connor, P. (2014). Open letter to Dr. Mark Emmert. Retrieved August 11, 2014, from http://www.milb.com/news/article.jsp?ymd=20140621&content_id=80915548&fext=.jsp&vkey=pr_milb&sid=milb.

Reagan, B. (2012). For D.C. baseball team, Deluge of Phillies fans is national disgrace. *The Wall Street Journal*, p. A1.

Reichard, K. (2012). Suns: Nationals forcing us to move from Hagerstown. Retrieved November 7, 2013,fromhttp://ballparkdigest.com/201202154522/minor-league-baseball/news/suns-nationals-forcing-us-to-move-from-hagerstown.

Ringolsby, T. (2014). Portland ready, willing and hoping for baseball. Retrieved June 18, 2014, from http://m.mlb.com/news/article/66946688/portland-ore-ready-and-willing-to-become-a-major-league-city.

Roberts, G. (2003). The case for baseball's special antitrust immunity. *Journal of Sports Economics, 4*(4), 302–317.

Solomon, A. (2012). *Making it in the minors: A team owner's lessons in the business of baseball*. Jefferson, NC: McFarland & Company, Inc.

Spurr, S. J. (2000). The baseball draft: A study of the ability to find talent. *Journal of Sports Economics, 1*(1), 66–85.

Spurr, S. J., & Barber, W. (1994). The effect of performance on a worker's career: Evidence from minor league baseball. *Industrial and Labor Relations Review, 47*(4), 692–708.

Winfree, J. A., & Fort, R. (2008). Fan substitution and the 2004-05 NHL lockout. *Journal of Sports Economics, 9*(4), 425–434.

Winfree, J. A., McCluskey, J. J., Mittelhammer, R. C., & Fort, R. (2004). Location and attendance in major league baseball. *Applied Economics, 36*(19), 2117–2124.

Winfree, J. A., & Molitor, C. J. (2007). The value of college: Drafted high school baseball players. *Journal of Sports Economics, 8*(4), 378–393.

Zimbalist, A. (1992). *Baseball and billions: A probing look inside the big business of our national pastime*. New York, NY: Harper Collins, Basic Books.

Zimbalist, A. (2003). *May the best team win: Baseball economics and public policy*. Washington, DC: Brookings Institution Press.

Index

© Springer Science+Business Media New York 2015

T.A. Rhoads, *The Call Up to the Majors*, Sports Economics, Management and Policy 7, DOI 10.1007/978-1-4614-8924-5

MIX
Papier aus verantwortungsvollen Quellen
Paper from responsible sources
FSC® C105338

If you have any concerns about our products,
you can contact us on
ProductSafety@springernature.com

In case Publisher is established outside the EU,
the EU authorized representative is:
Springer Nature Customer Service Center GmbH
Europaplatz 3, 69115 Heidelberg, Germany

Printed by Libri Plureos GmbH
in Hamburg, Germany